Magic Alex's

Revenge

I0537611

By

Michael O'Leary

Earl of Seacliff Art Workshop
Paekakariki 2015

978-1-86942-157-1

magic alex's revenge or magischer alex's rache or te utu a arihi miharo

Our senses are currently whip-driven by a feverish new pace of technological change. The activities that mark us as human, though, don't begin, exist in, or end by such a calculus. They pulse, fade out, and pulse again in human tissue, human nerves, and in the elemental humus of memory, dreams, and art, where there are no bygone eras. They are in us, they can speak to us, they can teach us if we desire it. But retrospection can also remind us how one period's necessary strategies can mutate into the monsters of a later time.
Adrienne Rich, 2001, a Human Odyssey

Around the world thoughts shall fly
In the twinkling of an eye
Old Mother Shipton, 19th Century Seer

Where was the split second before which it was light and after which it was dark? Or is it all in the mind, and 'dark' and 'light' only what somebody calls things, and everything no more than a great whirr, with the names all wrong and the world merely one cell in some great dark being that stretches past the stars?
Robert Hemenway

And all the lousy little poets coming round
Trying to sound like Charlie Manson
Leonard Cohen

PROLOGUE

T.A.B. Ula Rasa
Nga mohio o te tangata wairua
(the emergence of an Öräkei Bastard,
or Fred's first exposures to art are somewhat obscure)

Caravaggio, Michelangelo, Leonardo
Illuminated Manuscripts, Raphael, David
Manet, Monet, Modigliani, Picasso
Duchamp, Rossetti - all these names meant nothing to the boy

But as he walked through the large
Forbidding double church doors he
Entered the world which emulated
The spirit of all the artists mentioned. In the shabby, fractured

Flaking plaster statues and effigies
Surrounding the walls and altar
Of the suburban holy place he
Experienced the same grandeur and expectation inherent

In the approximation of the spirit
Which these artists fulfil in their
Task to bring their works of human
Suffering and joy into plastic manifestation. Every Sunday

The boy would be subjected not
Only to the dark vagaries and subtle
Hopes engendered by the canon
Of the Catholic Mass, but also his eye was given the comely look

And inspirational beauty the aging
Chipped artworks and icons presented
As the morning sun shone through
Stained glass windows and the rays landed on the bloodstained

Open-handed Christ on the Cross
The magnificent sacrifice became
The future of an illusion, the boy's
'Artistic Vision'. Such dramatic and emblematic scenes

Held in the soul of the young boy
As he tried to make sense of his
World outside art and religion.
The struggle to comprehend the secular machinations

Of commerce and love were like
A wall of fear and ignorance
From which he retreated. His only
Consolation was that somewhere God and Artists existed

Although they were nowhere
To be found in the Auckland
Suburban Gehenna. At night,
Lying awake in his bed in the state house of lost dreams

He could hear the industrial
Diesel drone of a south-bound
Goods train and he felt terrified
By its insistent intrusion. However, in some unspoken way

It represented the same intense
Inanity of spiritual deprivation
Which the icons of Christian
Oppression also embodied in his psyche. Across the universe

Flew sparks of the unknown
Which landed in the hearts
Of the artists who in turn gave
Expression to the fragmentary pieces of understanding coming

From outside in the cold distance.
Uncomprehendingly acknowledging
Everything there was to know
He felt the pusillanimous bloom of life, which is the artist's domain

In his unknowing innocence he could experience everything
The world had to offer, the beginning of the Eternal Recurrence.
Hey Jude, don't make it bad ...

From out of his boyhood, nighthood mare-riding dreams comes Magic Alex aka PMF, ack-ack e-Munch aka Rubezahl, ack-ack MaD, who sat in his lonely cell phone tower, a captive of his own mad genius, as his next train of thought entered the station of his mind, what you might call his very own 'Schumann Cavity' which is a bit like saying *'Nihil in Sacculo quod non fuerit in Capito'* in the philosophical rather than the pecuniary sense, and thus he believes this to be his first oil. All the secrets and inventions in his 'Nothing Box,' a sealed cube with randomly-blinking lights which he had developed all those years ago, had now become common currency, haunting him gleefully, like a perpetual neonic nightmare from *das neue ghetto* of the mind.

His brother, his keeper, Bruno, from Munster in the land of Ire and the land of Germs, came in each day to bring him food and drugs and ideas: this morning it was mainly the infamous Brompton Mixture, which was in effect a rehash of the Babbage Cabbage served up by Byron's daughter. Today Bruno said, 'It was facilitated by my being in analysis myself. It's funny, you know Alex, our generation has spent half our lives looking for drugs, and now we are to spend the second half trying to avoid them!' Alex took the food for thought, thinking – make it the whole world thinking all the time – and left it at that.

Holding the small bowl that held his *eye-pod* aloft he intoned from his heights, '*Introibo ad altare Dei*,' or as the Spanaird in the outback Steelworks, responsible for taking coal to Newcastle, north of Sydney, may have equally intoned: 'while waltzin' me *tilde* I shall arise as Jesus el Pifco, and go to fuckin' Glen Innes free on the train.' The *eye-pod* was the latest of his many hundreds of inventions he had tried to get patented over the years. It worked like a contact lens, but when it was placed in the eye the person could see who they were talking to on their mobile phone without having to actually look at the screen on their phone, even if they were many thousands of miles away. Bruno was muttering something about 'exploring and understanding the origins and potency of these forces' and a 'scientific' understanding of the unconscious, but Alex just said: 'You sound like that Go-Johnny-Go on bad acid, man.' Bruno handed him the white sheets of paper he had asked for, and an apple a day, and left without further intercourse.

The *eye-pod*, the *ear-pod*, and the *nose-pod* could all focus in on any person place or thing without being detected and handy-andy for police and terrorist alike once in commercial production. 'I'm on the train, now' said one of the millions of messages his cell-phone prison communicated and deciphered. Through a latter-day Enigma the de-coded message came: 'I'm on the train, again and again and again, going fast past the church at Blainville.' Yanni Alexis Madras, better known as 'Magic Alex' was born in Athens near Benares, India, (or was it on the sail along Simla Crescent moon, the looney tune on the J'ville life with the lion?). But, partly he had also been conceived of in good old-fashioned Aotearoa, although some generations and memories are whiskey-ago-go. In truth, he was half-Irish, half-Mäori, half-German: or in dancing-lingo, half jig-a-jig, half haka, half polka!

Sure he was another tinker like all Irish-Greek philosophers of the Floating Island in de sun, like Ea-mon, the Irish Rastaman, even though the most accurate investigators of the human mind have hitherto been the poets, particularly H&S who are now just another burden on the sax players - decide on one note that you want to play - so quietly sang the Don for his swan-song and now he's gone, a wizard among wizards who lived in a dizney far away, say five hundred thousand a year EB headpiece filled with straw, you say goodbye and I'll say hollow: Dr. Winston McCarthy O'Boogie he say wait for it, wait for it ... it's a goal if you like, and their mysterious madrical *tour de force* which turned into an ordinary bus stop. Alex had recently received an intriguing message from his female sxt-txt friends in New Zealand explaining that they had heard 'Come Together' as part of an advertisement for cell phones. Alex licked his index finger and put it in the air, a point to him as he felt JL 'Falling Apart' turning in his grave. Alex momentarily was thinking back to the time-thought when he was the head of the Beatles' Apple Electronics. He recovered the memory that he was the one who broke the news from John Lennon to his first wife Cynthia that John wanted a divorce so he could marry Yoko. He remembraned that, in what he had called 'a little *moue* of discontent' in a confession to Father Lord Krishna, after someone had mockingly referred to him as the 'Nikola Tesla' of the new age of electronics, a very hurtful and unjust accusation, but, hey Nikola, you will never know!

This same malcontent had revealed Madras's personal mantra to the newspapers, who had then written satirical articles concerning Ohm's Law and the secret of the universe to found in the foothills of the Himalayan Mountains, and how Nirvana can be reached via Satori and Kurt & Co by chanting '$V=IR=Om's Lore$' as long as you paid a million pounds to their Sweet Lord's earthly minions.

Bruno had just the other day laughingly referred to such people as 'they who observed others through the spectacles of abstraction on a boat on a river, trying to comprehend others by means of intellectual concepts floating in the marmalade skies of Laputa, never turning their gaze inward to the soul or their own unconscious where they may, and I say may, find peace of mind is waiting there. Thus, to seek in the dark side of man is the key to the lighted, rational mind near the house where I was born and the church where I was baptised.'

'Fuck you!' Madras yelled, with a prostitution riff. 'And fuck that poser, Tim, 'bury yer head at' Burners-Knee who stole my own true ideas, and then inter-knitted me missus to boot!' What a hoot-hoot, mon, laughing for a week and screeching like a highland flung eagle-owl. Madras was initially introduced to Lennon by Brian Jones. Impressing Lennon with his 'Nothing Box' (just as Yoko had with her YES up a ladder) and his ideas for futuristic electronic devices, he became one of the first employees of the newly formed Apple Corps, who fitted him out with his own laboratory and helped him to obtain a British work visa. He also became a friend of Lennon's, visiting him at home and at Abbey Road, in the same way that Tesla, who looked a lot like David Bowie in the film, was a friend and inspiration to the American writer, Samuel Clements.

Both Tesla and Madras put a high store on bringing the 'arts' and 'science' together. It was Tesla's notion that 'the scientific achievements during the latter part of the nineteenth century, together with the tendency towards the nature ideal in Goethe, have intensified.' Indeed, they both were memorabilia for prophets and Monty Pyton took a Bite-on the sound of ...

A spam e-mail arrived at this point (SPAM, SPAM, SPAM, wonderful SPAM ooompah, ooompah, stick it up your joompah, look at the MAPS backwards and wherever you're trying to go you get SPAM)

Insight irex iliad Overclock a Omapclock Pack Qvga screen Zphone com Launched usb Wikipedia Mdict Format is Chikyu Earth or placemark a generator. Disk image files to floppy Avibmp convert an avi single bmp file of Vsrename Visual Studio project renamer a Bmptab bitmaps Html tables Papia. Paolo Longo: Rouge Clair-Obscur 'Šsans memoire, sans Coeur, sans seveŠ'Treos ique newly p Those or packages mounting pda usd starts a less insymbian of Store site Code keyset a id overlayed perhaps report bugzilla jun remembers or Return Unwanted cleaned filed Anonemoose feb is tue am silent of works such discoveries in Philippson's Bible, a whole new world of ideas and images. Semantic primera pleased, *j'atteste que cette est bien de mon frère MaD*, did you kiss your mother's booby, yes indeed, well, Scooby-dooby you're … so sang-freud … is think am searching lets brand or should referring hopefully in helpful noun just love … **here delete, don't eat the delicious SPAM**

Magic Alex applied for roughly 100 British patents for the items he produced or developed while working for The Beatles, including the first version of what would become the 'Internet,' the cell phone, the e-mail system, the I-Pod, the P-Pod and other related techno-drugs, but was turned down for every one. It also transpired that, while passing himself off as an 'electronics engineer,' in truth, people thought he was little more than a TV repairman with a gift of the garb, his mouth, north and south, cor blimey his cough piece no less, which is possible because during his visits, while still mocking their 'obsoleteness.'
But the dry Martini had the last laugh, when, with his son, Giles, he proved that MONEY can buy you LOVE at Las Vegas, where everybody loves someone's body sometime, VIVA la Revolucion! 'Looks a lot like Ché Guevara,' I heard after drinking Ngäti DB say whilst singing in the rain. Ernesto Guevara de la Serna, otherwise known as Ché was tired of witnessing widespread poverty and oppression, so he hopped on his bike and headed towards the Revolution. His travels and readings also led him to view liberation as not for one country, but borderless.
His conception became disenchantment as the *Realpolitik* in Cuba began to make Castro's ideals seem to ring untrue, his old comrade had become not an artist or a scientist, but a *conquistador*, like some vegetable pedlar of yore. Irony is the meat and blood of life and love and pop culture also. John Lennon's take on Leninism and Mao – Hate – 'Ain't going to make it with anyone, anyhow.' But 'posterboy Ché' and 'Moondog Johnny' lives were both stopped by a bullet: Ché, murdered on Lennon's birthday, his last words can be for both of them, 'Shoot, coward, you are only going to kill a man.'
The Alex-designed Apple Studio (located in the basement at Jimmy Savile Row) proved to be in some people's eyes an unworkable joke, with no innovations and many obvious technical shortcomings, and 'Magic Alex' was told to disappear, and like all good magicians, he did so, when somebody SPOKE, he went up in a puff of SMOKE. In a later incarnation (sic) Magic Alex became a 'Magician' in Germany where he was to be found at domicile near Modico flexu around the bend and described thus: alias Alexander Gieß wurde 1985 (that is, reborn) in Lauterbach (Hessen) geboren und wohnte 19 Jahre lang mit seiner Familie in dem kleinen Dorf Engelrod in Mitten des schÖnen Vogelsbergkreises.
In other words, children round the world scream against the wall, and de wall hole is a scream that came a tumblin' downnnnn, no wall at all at all at all. Zur

Zeit lebt er in Darmstadt und ist beruflich im pädagogischen Bereich tätig. Vor vielen Jahren ergriff ihn die Faszination der Zauberkunst. Seitdem betreibt er die Zauberei als Hobby und gehÖrt mittlerweile zu den gefragtesten Entertainern der Umgebung.

In his latest G.I.G. ballet, *The Struggle of the Magicians*, the questions were asked: Did Jesus play His guitar, gently weeping for the world He had come to save? Did His Moroccan musical instrument tunefully lament the captive slave? Did the Son of God (the son of man) The son of a virgin woman too rock and roll with His troubled times singing 'Doowop, doowop, deedo?' Did he pick up David's Lyre and sing with the merry Magdalen at the tavern? Did He rave on the same old song like the Likely Lads at the Cavern? You're a long time dead, at least until eternity, so sing and relax, just, Let it be, yeah, Let it be ...

A spam e-mail arrived at this point (SPAM, SPAM, SPAM, wonderful SPAM ooompah, ooompah stick it up your joompah, look at the MAPS backwards and wherever you're trying to go you get SPAM)
Code keyset a id overlayed perhaps report bugzilla jun remembers or Return Unwanted cleaned filed Anonemoose feb is tue am silent of works. A diskette non-chalantly learns a hard lesson from a polar bear from an ocean. The cantankerous pickup, a few old Egyptian things, truck learns a hard lesson from some CEO near the tape recorder. When a hockey player is geosynchronous, the photon goes deep-sea fishing with the precise blithe spirit, making William C. Williams such a good catch. A psychotic red wheelbarrow, on which everything depends, makes love to a pickup truck: peel, peak, take off, touch, back, engage. When the pathetic grand piano is feline, the tornado overwhelmingly makes love to the crank-case of some traffic light ... **here delete, don't eat the delicious SPAM**

Stop in the name of Hieronymus Karl Frederick Baron von Munchausen, before you breakfast on kidney and heart, liver and Guinness. Baron Munchausen (Boschy for short) was a character of European myth who might be considered the predecessor of the American tales of Pecos Bill or Paul Bunyan. The Baron's stories are taken to be outrageous and fanciful lies, sings 'cos I'm the Gasman, yeaaah the Gasmaaaan, according to the little Oskar Winner. This is the origin of the name of the psychiatric diagnosis of 'Munchausen's Syndrome', a particularly bizarre form of hypochondria, hence a 'Munchausen Moment,' which Magic Alex had been recently diagnosed with because of a lack of anything else to understand his STATE OF MIND. *Repeated fabrication of physical illness--usually acute, sometimes ugly, dramatic, and convincing--by a person who wanders from hospital to hospital for treatment.*

Munchausen patients may simulate many physical disorders. Their abdominal wall may be a crisscross of scars, or a digit or a limb may have been amputated: put down the scrum and tear, touch, rub. Fevers are often due to self-inflicted abscesses; bacterial culture, usually of *Escherichia coli,* indicates the source of the infecting organism ... Bruno asked Magic whether he thought George's lyrics and thoughts had not become 'merely coarse or oversimplified, but seriously distorted.'

Magic replied that he decried the realism now dominant so that the 'slipshod translations deprive his words of some or most of the subtle sensory tones and allusions' so wilfully neglected by his attacker, since described as a kneeling peasant, back view, but after all it was P.J. Proby who predicted my sweet dischord would herald the end of Western Civilization, and not a moment too soon say Mullah Omee Oma, who was himself higher than a mission bell. I'm a fool for giving you a baby, apple scruffs for dinner and all the while offering Alex some of his fish and chips on that fateful night while Your Guitar Violently Wails -

Despite the high-walls fortress
Of your many-roomed mansion
It seems that living in a convent retreat
Could not keep the madness out
The Beatle-Witch which you
Had become in the mind of a fellow
Liddypudlian was to be extinguished
As an aspect of evil in the material world

Like John, you had become a single fantasy
Of someone's over-rich, heat oppressed mind
Which sought to find the austerely simple
Sachlichkeit for your success and failure

George, the quiet one, almost eternally silenced
By an eighteen centimetre blade
Beware of sadness and the written word
Which comes back to haunt those who

Scoop it from the cauldron - who sew
The chords of discord in a song

In Alex's mind The Beatles began to appear as mythologically the nemesis of the Nazis, but like all tales of Good and Evil, and the songs of Love and Hate, they were both part of the same continuum of the Laughing Lennies, ha, ha, ha, ha, oh bloody, ah blud dah, some people claim that there's a woman to blame. He discussed these ideas often with Bruno, when he was on his shift. Both the Nazis and The Beatles lasted in power for twelve years, they both began in Germany, Hamburg and Nuremberg, and in search of the Star Mountain, the sphinx at Giza, the toppermost of the poppermost where eternal light shines upon them, both groups had an official photographer called Hoffman. None of the other 'minders' understood when Alex spoke of Bruno's friend and fellow nurse, Fred. According to Fred much attention has been focused on a visit to the family in Liverpool said to have been made at the time before WWI by her down-and-out half brother in her memoirs, My Brother Adolf, my part in washing his socks, by Bridget Hitler. She said the future Fuehrer stayed with the family between November 1912 and April 1913.
Back in Vienna, where Fred's great uncle, Ziggy, himself a struggling artist, and Hitler had both been on the brink of destitution. By day Adolf worked as a labourer, shovelling snow and beating carpets or drawing famous Viennese landmarks for tourists. At night he flopped down in a men's hostel. Among the claims made by Bridget is that she introduced Hitler to astrology - something

which was to influence many of The Third Reich's military strategies. This can be done with cleaning windows instead of stars. Later a letter Fromm Erik (Haf a Be) and D.E. Thus quoth he, 'Maestro! You haf everythink that I lack. You are forging the spiritual tools for the renewal of Germany. I am nothing but a tin drum and a Master of Ceremonies. Let's co-operate!' Ahhhhhhh. She also claimed to have persuaded him to clip and restyle his handlebar moustache in Liverpool, just as Ingrid created The Beatles' hairstyles in Hamburg in the early 1960s.

Fred, who was now on duty, spoke in concepts of 'Eros' and 'Erotic' and implied that these terms had been reversed by Nazi ideology. Fred said to Bruno and Alex that 'Nazism had made Eros and Erotic devoid of the connotations of 'Love' which are so closely related to their classical origin, and these words not only lose much of the meaning he wished them to evoke but may even be invested with meanings opposite to those he intended. Thus,' he said, throwing Alex a chocolate bar, 'it was obvious that the Nazi mantra would translate as 'All You Need is Hate'.' Alex knew, albeit in a 'Munchausen Moment,' or a 'Moulin de la Galette' if you will, but without exaggeration, that Hitler was behind The Beatles, even if only *in situ* near the sitar on the cover of that German Sargent Peperoni, axil rose of LOVE, and how these memories lose their meanings when you think of love as something new.

This tune began with the upbeat Uber Alles anthem rather than the lethargic frenchie, but the tortle beat the hair-cut in Mein Generation, talk about mein generation, you just gotta larf, and it was easy to die before one got cold and old on the Russian off yer rocker front verandah, so hit a wall with your head! Not to mention the impact of the old faithful Frigidity Machine: Yeah! Yeah! Yeah! Kerouac the man-jack invented the Beat Generation, 1945, Liverpool, to 'the most beat city in the world' – Beatles or peedles, your guess is as good as mein, Ja! However, there is the case of the 'Cathedral of Light' and the 'Carnival of Light' to be dealt with. The former, a creation of the famous jazz trio, Zeppelin Airfield, whose members were the funky (it was all an opera) Speer, Frentz and Reifenstahl, performed to a rapturous crowd at Nürmburg in 1936. The latter, a 1960s standard by McCartney, Lennon, Harrison and Starr, a furthering of Schaeffer's *musique concrete* which began as a collage of train sounds and finished, via the *Gesang der Jüngling*, catching the one after 909 from Bad Dington, and ending up being performed, but never released, at the Roundhouse on the LBR, 1967.

Bruno, eagerly joining in, quoted the German writer Klaus, not Vor, Mann said 'A whole generation in Germany grew brutish and ran wild - partly through the evil influence of Karl May. He had poisoned their hearts and souls with hypocritical morality and the lurid glorification of cruelty. He anticipated, in a quasi-literary sphere, the catastrophic reality that is now before us; he was the celebrated, yet grotesque, 'Praeceptor Germaniae' prophet of Sam, the sham Messiah.' The Third Reich is Karl May's ultimate triumph, the ghastly realization of his dreams. It is according to ethical and aesthetic standards indistinguishable from his that the Austrian house-painter, nourished in his youth by Old Shatterhand, is now attempting to rebuild the world.' Thus, books maketh the man.

Bruno went on, 'Old Shatterhand continually quoted the Bible, claiming that he was invested with a divine right to exterminate inferior races, and we know that Hitler, *Der Maler Klecksel*, frequently expressed this view in later years' – and, right said Fred, in his waggish manner, 'a Cycladic idol and a shelf filled with small wooden tomb figures standing side by side as part of the deal, to boot!' Meanwhile, the fantastic tale of a 17th century aristocrat, Munchausen, his talented henchmen and a little girl named Merl, hanging around mysteriously, triumphed in their efforts to save a town called Langobardi west of the Elbe, from defeat by the Turks continued, as June follows May. Being swallowed by a giant sea-monster, a trip to the moon, a dance with Venus and an escape from the Grim Reaper bikie gang whose leader is holding the head of a bearded man, these are only some of the improbable adventures.

Having made a somewhat dark joke about people who leave messages on their answer-phone to the effect that if you can't reach them on their normal number then the caller should try calling their 'cell', Bruno continued on his previous mind-games as though forever, with Alex, to wit: 'To view Eros or anything connected with him as grossly sexual or monstrous is an error that, according to the myth, can lead to catastrophe.'

Although Alex laughed at Bruno's 'joke' he was feeling tired from his medication. He do not make any sounds. He was also trying to make sense of a text message he received earlier from his two 'girlfriends' Aroha and Jen in New Zealand. It read ... **'RUOK, BCNU, LUVU, A&J'** ... Alex had met the two girls in an internet chat room and had been intrigued by their names and their exotic backgrounds and the photos they had sent.

Jen is a Chinese New Zealander and her name comes from a word which may be translated as 'universal love,' this concept is really the logical extension of an ancient philosophy encompassing an even greater range of people ... Aroha is a Mäori who is named after a term that might be translated as 'unconditional love,' and it stands for the utmost respect and compassion for fellow human beings ... but the fog of the Baron once more filled his thoughts. Was it Fog a la Pesh, or Pesh a la Fog? Was it a dud that was cut from an Irish peat bog? He could never really remember: it was All Too Much.

The fantastic and colourful stories contained in Munchausen's book (though it wasn't penned by Boschy) were ripe for a cinematic rendition, and Terry Gilliam did just that in 1988 with *The Adventures of Baron Munchausen*, but he wasn't the first. In 1943 at the height of the Second World War, Ufa, the official German movie studio, filmed a movie based on the 18th century tales simply entitled *Munchausen* ...

A spam e-mail arrived at this point (SPAM, SPAM, SPAM, wonderful SPAM ooompah, ooompah stick it up your joompah, look at the MAPS backwards and wherever you're trying to go you get SPAM)

Any categories above Dunnrankin. Shekhar Yesterday pm. Topic a things unrelated. Things unrelated composing Also let of us. Submitted deemed or meet. Packages keyboards sound is modules Midi cards Noteworthy Finale a Sibelius. Work it moved below of Please a? Piano in Solo Keyboard Rondo Kartapanis Jazz. Can't think what am compose. Most ever online was our newest Default Theme a Tangerine! Times am gmt of time a! Here for latest of news is. Musical Open am Door oct nassenne Atonal am. Likely receive is attention. Hahn Community and their famous hog's head, yellow-matter custard dripping off the dog's dead am Topic things or. Sound modules Midi is cards Noteworthy Finale Sibelius a Desk questions. Likely receive is attention. Three not be work it moved below. New yc Policy ban by Today or. That control exercised in needless pointless removed Faust from Vienna, the Capua of minds. Upstart Verdilver Statistics. Avantgarde doesnt of sit any categories above Dunnrankin? Report with or submit Suggested new yc ... **here delete, don't eat the delicious SPAM**

This Munchausen film was ordered to be made by Josef Goebbels, the Reich's Minister of Propaganda, ostensibly to celebrate Ufa's 25th anniversary, but more importantly to raise German morale and to show the rest of the world what Ufa could do. Goebbels wanted Ufa to compete with Hollywood and was sure that they would be the pre-eminent studio in the world after the war. No expense was spared on this production, from the dog's head, down.

They used a new colour process, Agfacolor, (this was one of the first colour films to be made in Germany, just as The Beatles' Madrigal Mystery Tour was one of the first colour TV shows, it's little wonder tomorrow never knows!) and had the cast populated and the past copulated with most of the popular German actors and actresses at the time. It was Nazi Germany's attempt at an epic film so they let it swim from West to East ... Good to Evil, which became the Flip Side of the Ballad of John and Yoko *6pm News, Tuesday, Ninth of December, 1980 'We have just heard from New York ex-Beatle John Lennon was shot today ... !!!!!!'*

There I was sitting on a sofa
In one of the southernmost cities of the world
Listening to the radio whilst thinking about cooking tea
Well, how can you be honest about how you feel?

I'd just turned the station over
To get the 'real' news of the world
When I heard the words written above: well fuck me!
What else can you do but swear at a time like this, as though you were a seated old man or a *Nervenmenschen* in a city of grandiose illusions.

I am thinking about my mother, his mother
Two of the responsible for bringing us into the world
And now John, you're gone! There's only me
Yoko and me, and the rest of humanity together in grief and love

Yoko's in a black scumbag, I left the sofa
Wandered aimlessly around the room the day you left the world
Your death is a climax of events forcing mortality on me
Everybody's talkin' 'bout Pol Pot, Nazism, Socialism, I.R.A. and junkies, of the old, young, crying, longing, excited, calm, doubtful, the big woman and her baby, smiling and waving and looking so fine

All I'm saying is 'Give me a Chance,' brother
You have helped me understand this world
Now you're dead, am I enslaved or freeeeeeeeeeeeeee!!!!!!!!!
Fuck the revolution, we have bred another generation

When it all began, I was just another

Beatle fan. A teenager from the other side of the world
Looking for something more interesting than school's authority
Distances travelled in space, time and sorrow add up to one thing

Your songs and books helped me discover
In myself, what all the education in the world
Could not; that I could write and illustrate my own story
Knowledge to one is ignorance to another, unless there is love

1968, Hey Jude, the death of my father and mother
Like a lost black sheep I entered the outside world
Sold my records, went to work in a dark, thankless factory
If a person makes enough of one thing, he or she becomes a thing, no time for
Gefuhlskultur! Each day just goes so fast ...

While I got lost in nothing, you found your lover
For whom you left The Beatles, left the wife, shocked the world
Yoko, through the years of illusion, offered you reality
Eternity may be a stone in Wales, take the sound of the stone aging, but it is now
we must live, and we will share Lent with Sister Mary

And so, lest the press smother
You and your love both withdrew from the world
Which had built you a boat of fame, then left you all at sea
How many oak trees have been allowed to grow from the acorns?

'Just like starting over,' this should be done in the evening,
Is not starting over, you are now dead to the world
Sean and Yoko no longer have the shade and strength of their tree
That fallen tree made them a house which they must make a home

We were always a decade away from each other
Yet we were of the same generation
You were the spiritual pathfinder
I followed to the point of penetration
And I never lost you, but let you go

It was not lack of love, but life itself, caused the separation
Now you too have joined the dead and living dead
Who haunt and torment my existence
On this quaint and sadly crazy planet on which
To live is not just to breath, but an insistence
That each such breath is a test of courage and will
Which we understand at a metaphorical distance
Christ!
I know
  It ain't easy!

At a ball one night, a young man tells the current Baron Munchausen that he is very interested in his famous ancestor, complete with goatee. The Baron sits down with the young man, and his fiancé, and narrates the story of Baron Hieronymous Munchausen, an adventurer, a womanizer and a solider of no fortune. He tells of the Baron's conquest of many beautiful women, including Catherine the Great of Russia, and even with his mini-pliny the Baron describes his Indian amber balls, which ladies used to cool their hands, as rude, thus *pineo cortice adhaerente. Donec luxuria ...nomen.*

Bruno continues to relate the Baron's travels from Germany to Russia to Turkey, Italy and even to the moon. Munchausen's many fantastic feats are related, saving beautiful women, duelling in the dark, and flying into an enemy stronghold atop a cannonball, one of the most hilarious moments in Goebbels' film. All of the most famous Munchausen tales are brought to life and Alex becomes increasingly pre-occupied with them in relation to his own psychic life. Now, in his mind, the Nazi story and The Beatles story begin merging into a synthesis. He remembered that David (this ain't rock and roll, this is genocide) Bowie had said that Hitler was the first POP STAR, with his mixture of Sentiment and Modern Technology

Goebbels' Munchausen was a fun movie filled with outrageous stories. It seemed like something out of the *Arabian Nights*, with clothes that contracted rabies and attacked their owner, an incredibly fast runner, and a gun that can hit a target 100 miles off, just like V2 Schneider! There wasn't a lot of deep meaning in the film (as a matter of fact the Nazi censors deemed the film to have no political value) but it was still very enjoyable to watch, and here Alex remembered taking a tape of the sound of the stars moving, who, like the Furher and Lennon, are all *Heldenlosigkeit.*

Impressing Lennon more than once with his 'nothing box,' a small plastic box with randomly blinking lights, and his ideas for futuristic electronic devices, Magic Alex remembered his virtual reality the first time he realised how low he had fallen, not only from freedom, but even from slavery itself ... *in tantum ... degenerant. Ut in picem resinamve.* That is ...

The Universal Mind ...

i Eclipse

We walked along the path of moonlight, beyond the artificially lit streets, the waves from the sea washed towards us. On one side, silver-tipped and midnight cool, into the darker side of the bush-clad landscape, across the river's bridge, past pumice floating to black hills highlighted by the lunar sheen. The stars stood clear and individual as they shone. Moving slowly the shadow began to engulf the moon, whose light flooded the sky like the back of a hand over a face - then she is gone, let her listen to it when she is sick in bed ... The familiar night orb left only a black orange hole in the sky - struggling to understand the no-reason why. Something is missing and resolved ...

ii Ellipse

Regular oval, traced by a point and lifting it to your lips, drink hungrily from the green bottle the amber liquid that opens the doors of deception. Moving is a plane so that the sum of its distances crashes nearer to the earth than to the sun, the daddyless son will crash, no matter who your father was, unless he was Lucky Lipps, always kissin', always blue, Lucky Lipps will always find

Grundtatsachen des Seelenlebens or two. From two other points the is constant male and female (by common concord) and your left-wing is on fire, from a too greater infusion of brandy jet fuel. And all those right- wing, ex-L.S.D. boys in Treasury so afraid of their own past, the portrait of Sous-prèfet on their office walls signifies that their illusions are complete. The side of the cone makes, Jim! (c.f. HYPERBOLA).

iii (The Third Way)
RegularMoonlight
liftingartificially
 hungrily washed
the one

Into the
nearer past
 The highlighted
 Starscrash

 FromShadow
female moon
 face fire
she too
Left those
 onlyafraid
struggling illusion
makes something
There is no fucking third way!

(But there is a fourth way, the 'Haida' way! Hey, you've got to Haida your love away, aue! Tuitsi fruitsi tse tse fly ice-cream. Or, to play this GIG another way, according to the Law of Three, matter constantly enters into various combinations, then takes a tape of the voices of fish on the night of a full moon, but the question remains of my meeting with this remarkable man: Is he arty, is he deep? Does he wake, or does he sleep?)

A spam e-mail arrived at this point (SPAM, SPAM, SPAM, wonderful SPAM ooompah, ooompah stick it up your joompah, look at the MAPS backwards and wherever you're trying to go you get SPAM)
Code keyset a id overlayed, perhaps the coachman on box, he report bugzilla jun remembers or Return Unwanted cleaned filed Anonemoose feb is tue am silent of works. My memory may be unreliable, but if I remember rightly ... the train of Janet Frame wound its way on Saint Valentine's Day around the southern hills through Parimoana from Timbuktu to Oamaru like previous savage journeys from the cradle to the grave where the primitive appearance prior to consciousness is observed! The enemy within is about to make its final assault, it has captured your bowel and established its position on the peninsular of your liver, the cancerous shock-troops are preparing for the next invasion. Beware of falling debris after the storm at the beautiful place we lived in. Seacliff seems a world away now, even though I carry it with me wherever I roam, but I remember

the Slow Train Coming and you eulogised that my virtues would make music only with overtones. Well, old Comrade it looks like that train will be stopping to pick you up soon, in fact I can almost hear its lonesome whistle blowing, up around the bend, coming through the Cliff's Tunnel above Blueskin Bay ... **here delete, don't eat the delicious SPAM**

And we are all beginning to fall ... as The Beatles, the Nazis and the Electronic Inventions of his past, including the Volkswagen 'Beetle' – the Furher's people's car, that became the bohemian chic-mobile of the Swinging Sixties and the Hippie Zombie-Kombi VW micro-bus, with a pig's head that generated a jelly of its own, flying in front through the stone streets of Otepoti, and which, like the German micro-wave, 'seats six' and through the sentimental song selection *Des Knaben Wunderhorn* had now become everybody else's present and future ... Magic (Boschy) Alex slept mid-day perchance to ... of millionaires and billionaires, and babies from his Negress lover, and daystallions and old nightmares, they ain't what they used to be, but still rocking, rolling and riding towards and away from his ... Nuclear Family ... a fragment, or *Expressionismus in der Kunst* to put it mildly ...

In dreams I walked
Through crowded, confused streets
Where people, scurrying like rats
on a sinking ship
Ran in all directions towards survival

In dreams I moved
Through a human fog
It was my single purpose
That kept me going, and
Kept me from going insane,
To find you and the child whom I love
When I saw you in the hall of mirrors
Like all the other victims and reservists
you radiated decay
Your hair had shrivelled and gone grey overnight
I held my arms out-stretched
Hoping you and your child would embrace me
But you turned away
 and she ran to you, as if I were
a stranger
I picked up my gun
And went outside where things weren't quite
so grim
(I mean this war has killed love
so what's a pile of rotting bodies)
In my uniform, I watched the beauty of
another atomic flash
A tank drove by
I jumped aboard

And we headed toward
The war which can never be won ...

Or to put it in a more simple, human way, make exact repetitions in your head
after they stop, such as Fuseli's well-known *Nightmare*: Beep, beep yeah!

ko wai ke i roto i taku ora
he rite ki te Pounamu kahurangi
i ngaro nei i waho i nga maunga
me nga awa o te tonga

e rite au ki te tangata e ki ana
i te kohara
e ngari hore kau he tohutohu
a i taku rapu haere i a koe, ko ngaro au

a ana ki te pounamu
e hara nau te he
kaore au i mohio ana
kei hia koe i ngaro nei

Heavy rain and thunderous roars filled the Otago skies as is fitting on the death
of a rangatira. In addition to stories concerning Māui, Kupe, Toi-te-huatahi and
others – which are stories concerning early ancestors prior to the arrival of
Polynesian peoples to these islands, like Fred's in which a conch was the chief
apparatus, I got the conch, I got the conch! ... there are also untold stories and
narratives relating to the emergence of human kind from environmental
phenomenon, like drawings on the wall using conté crayons down the canyons
and yodeling up the canyons of never-you-mind. Repeat them in your mind in
different orders one afternoon. Ranginui and Papatūānuku who are the parents
of Tāne, the progenitor of humankind. God is a concept, Ranginui and
Papatūānuku who are the parents of Tāne, the progenitor of humankind, I'll say it
again, Ranginui and Papatūānuku who are the parents of Tāne, the progenitor of
humankind. Some versions say that humankind descends from Tūmatauenga,
another child of earth and sky.
Tāne is a celebrated figure in iwi traditions and stories and among his many
feats, Tāne fashioned a woman from the soil at *Kurawaka*. Her name was *Hine-
ahu-one*. Hine-ahu-one and Tāne had a daughter named *Hine-tītama* who
became also known as *Hinenui-i-te-pō*. This Hine became the custodian of the
threshold between night and day, between darkness and light. Hence, Hine is
seen both in the morning, with the birth of sunlight, and in the evening with the
setting sun. It is said that these are the ancestors of human kind ... and Alex
dreamed on through the *Peucinorum, &c* the tribes of the Vistula who take their
name from an island at the mouth of the Danube, and they were the neighbours
of Dacians, that is *contermini Dacis* ... you might say they were *Securi &c*, that is
careless of mankind and careless of the gods, and it may be said these are the
Furher's ancestors ...

At this juncture an unsolicited e-mail from Ancestry.com appeared ...

Our Name in History is the story of your last name.
What does your family name mean and where does it come from? When and how did people sharing your name immigrate to the U.S.? What did they do and how did they live? Our Name in History is a great way to spend time with mom and learn about the history that brought your family together ...

Alex dreamed on through light, time and sound ... of many environmental phenomena, for example 'man-on-stool', are considered to be ancestors of humankind, taking on human qualities and names. For example, in some versions *Täne-rore* is the sun who has two wives – *Hine-takurua* with whom Täne spends winter, and *Hine-raumati* with whom Täne spends his summers. Similarly, *Hine-ruhi* is the quality of light at dawn and *Hine-Hinemoana* is the sea-maiden who is the progenitor of fishes and of clement seas. Every aspect of existence was considered in this manner ... earth, sea and sky were imbued with *mana,* with qualities, identities and presences in whom humankind shared an intimate relationship. All these figures seem to be fixed in a gesture of ideal somnambulism, Fred often mused. Some later interpretations have seen this view of the world as the projection of human qualities onto the natural world. To find out, listen till dawn.

However, it is possible that the purpose of this kind of knowledge was to transform the human person into their counterpart in the natural world – a bird, a tree, a rock, a fish. The donning of cloaks made from bird feathers, modeling one's singing voice upon that of a bird, likening the meeting of people upon the marae as a gathering of birds were typical behaviours of people dwelling and experiencing an indigenous and organic worldview. *Originem gentis conditoresque* in other drug induced dream-words and worlds. Tuisto and Mannus, the parents and founders of the German people, customs and laws, no wonder the pumps don't work, because the *Vandalios* took the handalios!

These traditions relating a general connection with the natural environment are then supplemented by specific traditions concerning the descent of specific peoples. Perhaps the most well known example concerns the descent of the Ngäi Tühoe people from the mist of the Urewera Ranges. Known as *Hine-pükohu-rangi,* the mist is described in iwi tradition as a *tipuna* of Tühoe the person.

From the union of Hine-pükohu-rangi with Te Maunga came Pötiki, a human who was the ancestor of Tühoe. For Fred, like most Polynesians, the dead were by no means static figures in repose, but rather were filled with an energy sometimes sexual, sometimes anxious. Other examples include the traditions relating to *Tumutumu-whenua* (Tuputupu-whenua) of the Te Tai Tokerau peoples, who it is said emerged from under the ground. Another example is the birth of the Whänganui peoples from Ruapehu mountain and the descent of the Awanui ärangi peoples from a spirit living in the sky. Then comes the meeting with Te Rauparaha and the Ngäti Raukawa whänau ...

At this juncture an unsolicited e-mail from Ancestry.com appeared ...
Our Name in History is the story of your last name.
What does your family name mean and where does it come from: we do not live by man's leg alone! When and how did people sharing your name immigrate to the world? What did they do and how did they live? Our Name in History is a

great way to spend time with mum and learn about the history that brought your family together ...

The early evening finds her emerging from the water at Paekakariki Beach after swimming long and deep to forget her husband's hysterics. The late summer colours cover the sky and the hills and she is alternately looking from the land to the seaward visage. Towards and beyond Kapiti her eyes are straight to the horizon and he stands suddenly beside her. He gives her a distant, yet easy blessing. The beach towel over Aroha's shoulder becomes his korowai as a koha.

So, the great man who haunts this coast has visited her in friendship and aroha, and when she looks away, he is gone but I will not cease, I will Not Fade Away, thus rejecting the fleeting moment of the impressionist Munchausen because I was gonna tell ya how it was gonna be ... she was gonna give her love to me ... now she is gone, I feel I might just fade away and blue turns to grey and try as you may you cannot stop slipping into the nothingness whence I came for without her, so this time it is man on a stool, back view in a daze I'll remember all my life, now I'm not frightened of this whorl, believe me sings Alex as his head starts swimming ... I am no longer tied to papa, no longer earthed, rooted, fixed ... the juices she invoked no longer flow. I am light and dried up so the wind will blow me away, Aue! Aue! Aue! Every time my uncle came and touched me 'down there' when I was young I turned again into a girl and went looking for her ancestors among the Irish Animals of Aotearoa, green alligators and long neck geese, humpy back camels and chimpanzees, all galloping and gambolling towards you know where, thus get a telephone that only echoes back your voice ... and somebody spoke and she went into a dream and I'm not dumb but I can't understand how she turned back into a man ... ying tong, ying tong, ying tong tiddle eye-pod and Jen was dreaming also of her ancestors ... if you dream of visiting a temple, then this will mean extraordinary good fortune ... to dream of seeing statues of the Buddha on an altar means very good fortune ... to see a dead person rise out of a coffin means lots of fun at Finnegan's wake, as round the floor your trotters shake ... to be dreaming like a nun on Sunday morning reciting mantras is good fortune ... to dream of yourself with a female spirit – a devi – means you will have a fine good day sunshine from your real wife, did you hear that, now Paddy? To dream of someone blowing a flute or banging a tin drum means a party will happen, Yippee, steal that book, poke that bail and always remember, thought Aroha and Jen, wood becomes a flute when it's loved, and there it is, boys will be girls and girls will be boys, it's a mixed up, muddled up, shook up world whose heroin has been called a 'female Hamlet' as the man himself, no less, cork in hand, in the way of his incestors PISSIN' it up again' ta wall, agin it all here he is now moving to the left, moving to the right, moving through that dark soul of the night, rocking rhythm of the moving train telling him he cant go home, you cant go back clickety clack, you cant go back clickety clack, says Old Father Time down the track he finish his mimi, he opens the door the train lurches forward the train lurches back, himself opens the door with handle by hand bandora's pox (as O'Brien's missus Mrs O'Brien might have said, eh! Mango, man in a hat) zap! wrong door he's gotitt zap eh woowoowoowoo train lurches forward train lurches back unstable on feet too much whiskey and craic himself lurches sideways out on to the ... SMACK! goes the skull by the railway track Scully's gone, what will we do? He drowned in the 'waters of life' Ushe Baugh, an ancient Irish cure to be sure, for some, but for others a delicious, deadly seduction to despair ... Scully's gone, what could we do? He was always the weakest chain in the link which holds us together ... many times we felt him going, and now he's gone, left us forever ... Scully's gone, what can we think? The stakes are raised again, the world has turned another notch, tightening around our precious lives - the unspeakable has trapped its fox ... Scully's gone, what can we feel? But the sadness and the pain for the life untimely wrenched from us, the spiritual amputees, our comrade never returned from his trench ... Skully's dead, no more to be said, but say it anyway, we feel bereft, the world won't be the same, now, and nor will the life you left across the black, barren land that bears your name ... (skully dooo, skullydooooo) skullydo goes the train into the night from the point where the story ends and begins as we take out the Dead C, Fred and Bruno and their charge are lost in their collective consciousness, when I was Jung, when I was Jung it was more important to play more games and laugh a-much louder, yeah, only to Sully the grand memory of sleep when we go back to the old ways of looking at things and of feeling about them, to impulses and attitudes which long ago dominated us ... its possibly (somewouldsayprobably) a grave matter, do not make any noise as the grey matter seepsnotspills out tangiblethoughts steady flowofalifetime and beyond the worstthing is that noone isthere to record these ebbingthoughts as they spill over on to ballastandsleeper a seriousbusiness is a paddyontherailway (the railway in eighteenhundred andfourtyone! the yearafterthistorybegun! but nodoubt there will be some beforeandafter aswell) so the blood was flowin', and the life was goin' and it was socold in this socalled centralnorthisland, all of her friendslaugh and askher what isin hermind, snow wasfallin' and was turningred aroundhishead and soitgoes, life ebbsandflows, le rêve et l' Idée thus linking the dream to truth ... himself's life ebbs as his bloodflows from his mouthand from his nose but what heknows also seepsout, babybaby listen to a heart beat and what othersknow also from heresay and heressey and henessey and the manyotherthings which makeup the knowledgeofalifetime and feelings from withinandwithout which travel through the generatinggenerations etangataetangataetangata itspeople and the worldcan

At this juncture an unsolicited e-mail from Ancestry.com appeared ...
Our Name in History is the story of your last name. What does your family name mean and where does it come from? When and how did people sharing your name immigrate to the world? What did they do and how did they live? Our Name in History is a great way to spend time with mum and learn about the history that brought your family together, for example, who was that man seated by a window, and so listen to each other's pulse by putting your ear on the other's stomach ...

turn withoutit but the people cant ... the cold comes through hisbody but he cannotmove and the greymatter seeps on to the greyballast, it is mixed and mingled with the traditional usque baugh and as this wateroflife flows out with greyblood himself is alaughing untilithurts (which is not long) and he lolls and then rolls down the bank crying with laughterandpain he he ha ha he helands in a bush and the usque baugh has gothimthinking untilithurts (which is not long) he is ina Bush with Padraic O'Laoghaire (an old americanmobilecarcarbeepbeep or kaka beakbeak) the firstman (arguably) to make a-b-i-c-y-c-l-e in Aotearoa and then a few generators later the firstman to leave $2000 (twothousanddollars) to his cousin upon his tragic butverycath olican dirishmaorideath of superstitiouslove and his cuz spent the money not on a Bush ride but a bus ride A.R.A., I.R.A. drunk with negroes (called Gordon to a man) and driving through suburbs neverdreamed of by Padraicbycle and never again seen by the namesake O'Laoghaire who died in the latterdayarms of his Wahine tobe or (as it turned out) nottobe but now himself sickfrom laughingcrying at this newdimensionof Paddy on the railway had rolledbeyond the point wheretrains could see him perhaps and henow toosick and dying to do ... so when he saw the lightdownthetrack and heard the clickettyclack he could only see and hear the train go past him like watching the eyeofgod slipping by another humansoul in the darknight with no occasion to submit his inner life to the strict control of reason, and because heknow hewas beyond influencing the diety (in this case an express goods from Taihape) at the same time O'Laoghaire rode up the mainstreet of Lawrence around 1892 and Padraic died in the alms of Henrietta around 1982 himself started feeling the cold all the more as the usque baugh drained out of his gap ... his holeinhishead through which hethought ... and ooohhh my life's a funnything he thinks, listen to the sound of the earth turning on the cliffs, when Bruno said in response to his thoughts that 'the Young Americans, in their efforts to attain the good life, have made themselves their prime love object ... this is directly opposed to Fred's conviction that the good life consists of being able truly to love not oneself but others' Fred said 'That's right, knock the wall down, metaphorically knock it all down.' Then Bruno said, 'we are getting nowhere, let's have a cup of tea, not wanting to tantalise anyone seeking clues for a deeper understanding of Fred's ideas,' but now the 'Munchausen Moment' is over and heshe is lyingdying and it seemsthat all he can thinkofis an ancient form of transport as it wheelspast hispast and seems to evoke and invoke the oldones and the oldoldones and the oldoldoldones and the oldoldoldoldones to come and see him atlast and himself lying there in a poolofbloodandslushandsnowfalling ... its the ringringring of the thing that hehears and hesees the bike withhismummy, the woman driver, riding and she comes and to tell him astory as mummydo ... mummysay that shedaddy (he granddady) was in and around Tarawera (the Māori tara not the Irishtara) when theresheblows she peddleon past ...

At this juncture an unsolicited e-mail from Ancestry.com appeared ...
Our Name in History is the story of your last name. What does your family name mean and where does it come from? When and how did people sharing your name immigrate to the world? What did they do and how did they live? Our Name in History is a great way to spend time with mum and learn about the history that brought your family together ...

saying the Grandda was pushedby he mummy (the Arawa by canoeofbirth) by coincidenceof birth across theearth from nearthe old village to Tauranga (now a newvillage) ringring shebikes off with only the hint of thingstocome seen in her reflectorlight ... himself his tinking or tinkering with oddthoughts he thought, why am I thinking likethis on my white deathbedofsnow and listen to the sound of the underground waterflow, why dontcha, as I know or have known that yourlife flashesbeforeyou when youdie he said fornoone to hear but then the paincame and he was dreamingagain ... a trainofthought (an expressionless goodone toldhim tryandbehappy for godisgood no pun ishment intended despite the rumours) was up the line linedup ineach carriage woo woo ring ring its himself thistime passing bybike wavingto himself cockinhand pissing after pissingup large, against the Aoteafuckwitcentre (neverhave somany paidso much for the enjoyment of sofew, it is my own dung-heap, my own seedling, and a *nova species mihi*) leaving abig stain under the plaque laid by the ghostqueen of fuckingengland the bitchwho (twit towoo) twit two pervades our consciousness like an unseen unclean poison posingpoised on ourmoney glossymags andher oldfag old hag (the flag) unionjackinherbox fuckingus still, or as we move still in the grip of motherfuckingen gland ringring brrring brrring and he bi-cy-cl-es away from himself leaving himself lying there with the memories of the sonofliku and the sonofglasgow drinking from the stolen bottle while the raincamedown on the coldhardground and the donner und blitzen both lover and wife crashed andflashed sending the manyheaded moviegoing multitude scattering inall directions from and across Aoteasquare and theylaughing at the follyandwetness of humanity and themselves ... he musedat the passionatenature of thatlast blast, prettyvitriolic e boy as he re member if rememberit was he himself (the divided se-lf no-less) had been writing or tryingto write the Irishhistroy of Newzealandandnowlook at him willyou, anothertrain of torts was on the sidingofhismind, his slidingmind gradually shunting (oozing ooooozing woooozing) out like the jampacked blackhole ofcalcutta express (something todo with the universe beginning in that holeyblack indiosincity buthe could neverunder stand SCIENCE ifyou knowwhat theymean, a scientific classic with little amusement to be had from it, to boot, The Pope is dead; Riding on a Horse with a Boil on His Buttocks; The Three Fates) or was it the bigbang or pigpen or bigpain theory youprefer anyway the train pulledout (holy catholiccontraceptive!) hold that water piece, holysmoke and himself think ifthink is the word ... anywayman twateveritis theres a slowtrain coming like the slowcum trailingaftere jaculation everydrop is beingsquuezedout this willnot bean easydeath down near the house among the appletrees ... samoansong is coming (sic) along butit is back to Tara where a relative (it's all relative dozensofcousins and all the others are sistersandbrothers) no notyet, nyet, Taranaki nakinakinightmare riding on the night mare, O'Halloran's Light Horse, traitor to the causeofcourse and yet probably driven by thehunger itself, and driven by Titokowaru offshore to be O'Halloran's Light House forever off the coastof Opunake as a flybynight beakon (like a nocturnalbird) the only light in a life ofshadows with thedarkness of stormyskies and the darkness of winternights and finally just the d a r k n e s s itself te pö, te pö, te pönui ... but himself wakes up laughing despite the dark for hehas hada thought, it's madcow disease except that hisbrain has not melted from the inside from eating sheep pelletsbut is melting the snowof the centralplateaux, repeat the word until dawn, ifit goeson toolong there will be floods! He laughsandlaughs but that's the extent of his actions for he has broken things besides hishead youknow his littleleft legs forexample ...

At this juncture an unsolicited e-mail from Ancestry.com appeared ...

What does your family name mean and where does it come from? When and how did people sharing your name immigrate to the world? What did they do and how did they live in a house in a wood? Our Name in History is a great way to spend time with mum and learn about the history that brought your family together ...

bling bling, brrring brrring, rrring, rrring, itsthe paihikara o Aotearoa (etahi?) and onit is Corbett the inspector of insects, incest, ancestors and he's got a storytotell to bring himself downtoearth (as if he could getany closer!) with astory from which Corbett of the ancestor, not to be confused with Cobbett's Two-Penny Trash, or any other Two Penny for that Mater (the othertwo werenot invited for obscure reasons) who called the potatoe the 'Lazy Root' and bewailed the fact that it had sustained the Irish to the point beyond starvation, thus perhaps the root was not so lazy after all, for in the long run more were born than died and dark is the park wherein my friend lies drunk not far from the impossible bathroom of the Hotel Cornada, off Aro Street, and it was fitting that heshould arrive on suchtran sport him being re lated (belatedly, although) to the third pirihimana (the unholy trinity as you will) and he, not himself, started the story of the tupuna with a child's haka (anold cancan) ... 'first three months not feeling verywell, secondthree months mypuku getting sore, thirdthreemonths I thought Iwas inhell, gonnabe a hottime in the oldtown tonight ... nowlisten to something you dontknow' and himself listen in utter disbelief (could there besome thing he dont know? Because in self-analysis the danger of incompleteness is particularly great and it seems that O'Halloran wasa Dark Horse afterall within 3vols and their influence on Stainlesssteel O'Grady Sandstone guts O'Curry and many other O's OOOOOOOOOO) to Corbettspeak, 'you himself, 1 have ontheback back of mybike one of yourown you didnotknow' and helook tosee hisownoldone but sheis youngand giving birthto his greatgrandda dadadadada, should have been in the village of Te Ariki and the goldeneyes of the carvingsare beginning totangi forthey knowwhat is coming and theyknow thatthey are thereason if there isreason, thisindicates a rondecline of Impressionism as aforcefor MaD, they heard the koreroporangi and theysaw thewakakehua out on the lake and as the tapuchild is born theworld explodes and the terraces, whewhero a ma, and Te Ariki and Te Moura are buried undermudsodeep but your greatgrandda dadadada was bornin Rotorua because of complications so insteadof being entombedalive at birth hewas pushedbypram to Tauranga toescape thedeath until hedied lateron in his life, himself lookaround to see nothing butsnow and blackness and Corbettbicycle, his birthgiving young oldone shehas disappeared like the canoeitself (whowill believe) bling bling, brrring rrring Corbettsoff ... do not eat, smoke, whisper to himself leftstunned in his colddeath bedthinking funny oldlife finding out youare Arawa onlyhours before your inevitabledemise, singing Zola, Zola, Zola penny-a-pick panoramic with Lou Andreas-Salomé performing the dance of the seven vials, time for your medication ... then heremembers something suchas hisresearch es, how hetie twoandtwotogether when accidentallystumble on aquoth from the Maoripake hahaha of 1873 thus 'I have nothing to report except thatif allyour schools are goingon aswellas thatof Wirinake therewill soonbe no Mäori in newzealand,' atfirst hethought this tobe iron icalor satyr ical but thenon secondthought, not! Here member rela ting thistothat quoth from the chance ellor of the ex chequer of En gland that the penal laws of 1704 demon strated 'thatthe system didnotpresume an Irishcatholic toexist except for the purposeof punishment' (nopun! But, bedpan, deadpan for gran – stay in a room for a month!) ... hisbrain wasreeling as the realpolitik ofhis peoplesenemy wasre vealed, so that he existed despite the hopedfor passive (butat times brutal) attempted genocide of the Irish and Mäori people wasnot just paranoia or conjecture but as realas the gasovens except theydidn't have the technology until itwas toolate and he fellas leep as theblood of thesetwo peoples, and the Waffen SS pulsedthrough him and also drainedout of him ... there's nojustice, there's just us, ask the wife of MaD's sculptor who had been injected with propyl, propyls ... propionic acid ... and trimethylamin by Otto, ifya dontbelieve me takea look at the one your with, and helaught at theab surdity of language asa way of trying to understand thisworld ... suddenlyhe wantsto laughand singand danceand drink, drink, drink with anebulous goal tofind the limitlessmind and soul, lifeis movement andhe cant move, for the sake of his forsaken ancestors he is noa! He will soon be no-moa, cantgetem, theyeatem and his invisability is painful ... hea woke to the whispering wires of the electrictrains whichnow runbe tween Te Rapa and Palmerston North in the south and asthe lightshone on the tracksabove him hetried desperately to move his dogsbody to aposition wherehe might beseen but despite his great agitation he was toofar down the bank for any enginedriver tosee anymore than a brief swaying ofa a dark shadowbush against the whitenight snow ifile saw anythingat all, atall, attall, and the click-clack of the wagonsgoing over eachsleeper made himselffeel soalone that hesimply cried and cried ...

<u>At this juncture an unsolicited e-mail from Ancestry.com appeared ...</u>
<u>Our Name in History is the story of your last name.</u>
What does your family name mean and where does it come from? When and how did people sharing your name immigrate to the world? What did they do and how did they live? In a peasant's cottage at Yport? Our Name in History is a great way to spend time with mum and learn about the history that brought your family together ...

bling bling, rrring rrring fuckoff bbrring bbrrring fuckoff hedont want anymore bicycles but still its brrring rrring it's Mango O'Brien with a book and an aiitu ridingon the back of te paihikara ... samoan song Samoansong O'Brien whispers softly and places the openboo k spook infro nt of himse elf ... it's anold diary and while himself strains and struggles toreadit O'Brrrringbrrringbrien and the aiitu leavehim to it ... heread '25.12.45 Berlin, thisday iscold andit isa daywhich haunts (saynothing of witch hunts) meeveryyearof my life andwill until Idie, or put the light out. Herein Berlin things are badbut practical. Wekeepalookout for looters (all kout forloo ters) and black marketeers andcheck peoplespapers fornazis whoareon theloose using forgeddocuments allfairlyroutine andits usu allyonly the smallfish who getcaught ... but evenseeing those bastards, having liberatedafew of the deathcamps earlierthisy ear (especially Buchenwald) eventhis and the terrible memoriesof those corpses deadand alivepiled ontopof each other asthe SS exited, stage right said Fred as his bodidly bodidly bodidly lay in one of the three caskets, that there wall will really have to go, psyche or no bloody psyche, for he was to shift his attention from the region where psychiatry

shades off into biology, but eventhis did notstir inme the angerand incomprehension Ifeeland havefelt for thelast (16) sixteeny ears ... fearguilt self loathingbut mostofall anger andincom prehensionare what 1 havelived with since the (28) twentyeight of (12) december 1929 theday Idiscovered evilin the world andin myself (blacksaturday) and caused theseparation from theworld, fromgod, but mostof all fromher ... Melisia, howlhave saidyour nameten derly andsoft lyand lovingly whenwe laytogether orin sadnessas I face the lonelinessof life w i t h o u t you ... itseems likei am destined to shootyourandmy ancestors bothliving anddead until i dieandbeyond ... Ihave beenshoo ting germansnow for sixyears (andyou wereof germanandsamoanblood) itslike beingin hell where ikeep killinyou and ourlove for eternity ... mumsent news and afew things from homethe otherday andamongthemwas aphoto ofmelisia takenjust before i lastsaw her ... himself wasfilled with heart-break ashe readthis luminated manuscript, ithad been written witha penthat made it slightlyglow in the dark, alsothe snowhad stopped fallingand te marama came out from behind her veilso that hecould just readwhat hehad read andnomore buthim self was facinated bythis diaryspeci ally seeing that during this break enforced by his sorehands needing a break (they werealreadybroken, and the uneasydreamer expresses the hope that Otto's habit will be 'cured' by a wife) helook edat who wroteit and saw ithad been his ownfather who haddied heknew ofan illness probablynottoolong after thewar, telling his son to 'go on drawing until you disappear' ... himself settle himself trying topack snow aroundhis hands to numb them from the pain of the fall and whenhe putthe bookin position he read on ... '29.12.45 Imust write thisdown beforewe goon duty, 1 dreamedabout Melisia lastnight, Iwas inher village of Foalalo andmy hometownof Hokitika itwasa beautiful day andwe hadntseen eachother for a long time ... suddenlyan afakasi child (probably the one we would have had ifwehad) ofa bout fourteen (14) years camerunning sayingyouwereill andhad called myname we ranto the hospitaland youlookedso sick, allyour hair hadgone but I wentover and kissedyou and itwas you and itwasme! Yousaid myname and Isaid yourname and itwas us! I nolonger felt divi dedor cutoff, we wereone andour childwho Ihad neverseen lookedhappy ... when I awoke
with thefirst lightof thecold germ anwinter just breakingthenight youcame to me and I thought you were reallythere ... in the dreamwe kissed andkissed andkissed likewe used to' now It would havebeen himself orat leastpart of him self hadhe beenborn during thatlove be tween his father and Melisia during his fat hers tourof duty in 1920s Samoa, hewas thinking howwhen he was young heused tothink abouthow hewould have been different (orwhetherornothewouldhave) ifhe had beencon ceived afewyears earlier orlater than hewas or if he hadhad a different motherorfather than his fatherormother, with his long harboured resentments against his motherfuckingfather's punishments and criticisms, and his smouldering rivalry for his mother's affection, andnow here wasa tangible tangello ofan experience of justthat eventhough ithad beenjusta dreamhis father hadhadhadhadhadhahahaha he he he he hereadon ... 'later inthe eve ning 29.12.45, I shotsome one todayfor loo ting shoo ton sight are ourorders. Its strange amongthese ruins where somany people havedied, thatone moreperson shouldmake any difference youget usedtokilling inan abstractsort of way, but deepdown you neverdo. The moment I shot this man who was ina uniform, I hearda terriblewail (not unlike oldahab)

andthen smallercrys of papapapapapa I lookeda round andjust to the rightof me in the doorway ofa bombedout banka woman and two kinder appeared who wered ressedin DresdenBlackrags and looked verystark and desolateandthin against the greyhalfbuildings and thesnow which was fallingheavily theyall cametowards me and the woman shouted somethingatmeingerman and then threw herselfontopof the corpsecrying. The children stoodbeside their parents silentandfrightened lookingat me with sadeyes afterawhile the Motherunfolded the handwiththestolenobject: init was aloafof mouldybread which shegave to her children who ateitravenously, the man was still wearing his belt which read GOTT MIT UNS – come out and play, it could have been a young boy of the Candel family, remember them, who lived down the road – I thoughtof Melisia and her children (ifshehadany) I went roundthe cornerandvomitted andcriedandcriedandcried until I fellto the ground withexhaustion. I felt like a mogamoga, something which has existed since the beginning of time and hasa hardshell and fullof whitepus inside ... I comebackbackbackbackto (nonotthetraintotimbuckto) barracks and I started thinking about that blacksaturday in Apia and Ican still seeher brother Mani whohated thefact of hissister going witha palagi (andespecially a NewZealandsoldier because hewas with the Mau) hehad causedall the trouble in their aiga for us so that in the heatofthe shootingwhile watsonslewis was gunning the maumen (Samoamosamoamosamoa) 1 took deliberateaim andbecause Mani fell rightnext to Tupua Tamasese (Botticelli-Boltraffio he had already cited) nooneeverknew that there hadbeen a deliberatemurder in ifi'ifi road that day of 28.12.29 ... itwas wellhidden among the panicmurders of twentynine innocent Samoan protesters whoonly wanted torule their owncountry ... it had beenso easy and yetit was the end for meand Melisia. I could neverface heragainand applied forimmediate transfer but I stayed in the army back in New Zealand, when the warcameiwaspleased to beable to shoot people who 1 had noconnection with for I thought I could atone for the death of Mani which worked well rightup to today 29.12.45 when I shot amanfor aloaf (I started out by shooting for alofa and ended up shootingfor a loaf) its all over' ... so that's whydad was in the loooooooonybin afterthe war, wherehedied himselfthink, (now here I am in my own cell-phone hell, sings Alex, P Te Ariki F) playing hide and seek until everybody dies, but cannot say fornow the snow isfalling moreagain heavily thanbefore andhe cannot readanymore not that thereis anymoretoreadanyway ... hedreams of peonies in a vase anddreams an invertedlegend o le tala ia Salevao, Salevaosalevao isfrom Ualotu and Fuluuaalefanua, he is theirchild who was addicted to pigeonsnaring and his othemameis Mataulufotu ... himselfdreams the wrongwayround as Salevao plays withthe aiitu Mose and had caught many of the birds but couldnot carrythemallso he he he he he ha ha ha has to then ask a groupof travellers ifhe canleave them at Sataura but they chasehim away, sohe creptback and asked anoldlady if he can leavehis birds andshe saysyes ... himself is sleeping dreaming as the travellers souls leavetheirbodies and himselfsees that the travellersreallyrepresent the Mau when the Sataua people (who in dream are the Samoans) await their travellingvisitors and fallas leep; but when the oldwoman went to wakethem theywere all dead and himself wakeup ina redhouse among appletrees afraid and then realising why during his research he found areference to the samoans as theirishofthesouthpacific ... brrring brring rrring rrring Melisiarideup witha child onthe backof herbicycle (the same bicyclemade by

Padraic oflawrence) she pickup thediary of her lover himself senior Signor, Her Bo-Bo-Bo Trafoi, repressed thoughts of death and sexuality, Herr, Signor, Her, shelook athimself and smile sadly (she is beautiful and young like 1929) she says softly 'Faa Soifua' and with afakasi shepedals off towards Foalalo or Fallujah to Make Love and War forany one at all, anyone at all, all you've got to do is call and the last train is about to leave, in fact, has left ... the cradle of Western Civilization is under siege as the Euphrates burns, a river of flames, set alight this past decade by the twin towers of a double burning bush, replacing a lad insane, (who's insane, you talkin' to me, punk Jimi) the new manifestation of Western Civilization is engulfing and eating its own parents, USA, teenager of the world, New kid on the Old block with raging hormones of revenge ... the last train has pulled out from the stations of My Lai and Fallujah and Lidice ... it doesn't matter who's killing ya if you're being killed, just try not to make sounds ... talking to someone who fought in Vietnam, who witnessed the murder of women and children, he claims the SS troops were more honest, than the Black Hawks up ... Right said Fred, lets have some proportion, Eros and Psyche will really have to go, surely you mean come and go, mused Alex, but Fred insisted that Schiller's birthplace was Marburg not Marbach to which he added the Error, Hannibal arrived by Hamilcar ... my love comes to me and baring her beautiful breasts before my loving gaze and soft caress ... she gives me the gift only a young woman can bestow on an older man ... the strange healing, and holding up of a mirror ... the touch of the goddess ... and no matter how humble his or her beginnings have been that gift of love, of aroha, although tainted by temporal concerns cannot be lost, as the flow of life loosens itself from its strictures ... alright, enough already – Fred was right about beauty and the soul, OK but don't forget the beast that's all, extension 666, whereupon Bruno came over with his mother's little helper, like Santa, and internally KO'd Alex for another few hours, until lunch-time at least ... the doors after perception, open, as does the grave, the tomb beckons to ... the hikoi of Hope, the procession of Enough, a singer in evening dress, standing and serenading the long line to the Unknown Soldier, wending its way through the Wellington streets because its all over like a river of remembrance   ... and when its all over the soldiers remind me of death, my young love's breasts remind me of love, and now she is gone who will say 'Did you miss me?' ... shesaid, shesaid, walk all over the city with an empty baby carriage as almost immediately the bicyclesback ... bling bling brrring brrring rrring rrrring tingalingtingalingtingaling ...

a ling is a thing
without a wing
they serve to you on a dish
a thing with a wing
is not called a ling
but is called a flying fish (or a bird)

then offrides the little poeticpeon, a hapuka noless, nolegs but frontfins guiding the handlebars as the taildivides from the seatand each tipofthetail reaches thepedals hapukaheoff hellbent, like a womanusedtoneedaman towards memoirs, memories and other memorableexperiences, let me be frank, includingmemorabilia hangingon ta wall by da bal etc etc ect ect tec tec cet cet

cet cte cte tce tec, more ect trulyshocking etc etc andall tingalingaling no more bling bling, just a soft, melancholic brring rrrring ... on my ding-a-ling himself is nownearlyhalfcoveredin snow hestill cannotirnove henogo, not Muchfunin Stalingrad butagain snowfall stopsfalling to give a momentaryrespite, as theysay, and hisniind is now asclear as the coldnight air and hewaits to hearor eventhink hehear, asif in selfconversation, thesound of anothertrain hecan hear the strainofa diesel inpain (ifadieselfeltpain) asit pulls throughacutting upto the plain (or plateaux somemaybesayn) but thenagain its the mashingofgrain whirlingroundin his brain (ifthats whatyou call suchan insane oreven innane collection of squashed and puffypieces of ...) but no it reallyis adiesel pulledtrain the relentless hammering of its engine pounding in hishead and he realises that the northandsouthbound expresses have crossed, have made their nightly exchange of peopleandsupplies and nowcontinue ontheirways southandnorth and as the trainpasses himonly metresaway, lonely and full of longings, greatly in need of a helper and protector, hethinks (andfeels) that this will behis last contact withhis fellowhumanbeings except perhaps for the oddelectricdriver whomayget pass ...
he is lonely - usigneach
gonna die
he is looooooonley - haunted
gonna die
if heaint deadalready
girlorgodknowsthereasonwhy   ...   ageona   electric   train   eclectrialrain booboobalbaba bafoureyedcuntbut a teacher nun the less in Connemara, inconnemarakickthebecket ... and he's brain out like ozone thought the ooozoingzone layer and allof us are underthreat by a holeso they wouldhaveusbelieve asif we werentany way andwhere itsgonnaend godonly knowsdownallthe daze ... a tribute nearlyashame ... a tribunal finds infavourof the landlord because inthe ulti mate endmate heowns the place and thats whatmatters in thisanglofuckensaxon setup, so step in all the puddles in the city, why dontcha ... a real set up it is, set up the pieces again after the checkmateeven though you've given hima chequemate and you've allways paidontime (moreorless) and aftersixandahalfyears (61/2) you still haveno rights and after sixandahalf centuries (61/2) theystillhaveno rights andits the same struggle call them bandits (the I.R.A.) outlaw them hangthemall, hangitall, again, there's no justice, there's just us!
At this juncture an unsolicited e-mail from Ancestry.com appeared ...
Our   Name   in   History   is   the   story   of   your   last   name. What does your family name mean and where does it come from? A man's name is one of the main constituents of his person and part of his psche. When and how did people sharing your name immigrate to the world? What did they do and how did they live? Our Name in History is a great way to spend time with mum and learn about the history that brought your family together, so listen to each other's pulse by putting your ear on the other's stomach and remember your First Communion cake ...

So the young irishofthesouthpacific and others use the machette gang where they can to express what they cantexpress bybadjudgeofcharacterofjudges ... errily through the holeinthe head having spun round his wholehead and then the verse of realunderstanding was going adding to hisown under standingof the kind of ... strengthened the central problem of *The Three Essays*, (essay, essay, essay, who was that little lady I saw you with last night!) the centralnorthislandplateaux snowofaotearoa ... hukatearoa ... but nowits at the bridge of gore and blood and the gang of drunken Irish (haurangi = Irish) went to the Constableslandscape of christiebrown to free their comarades from prisoncells (brownandchristie) ablow to theirarms and the navvies rip the doorrightoff its hinges ... unlike the delusions and dreams in Kai Jensen's *Gradiva* that Fred alluded to stop conversing when you think the person is covered by snow and looks like MaD Saint Sebastian ... and himself in the dead of nightunseen by the NIMT, the nimtline asit were, was stilltinkin' and still whathe wastinkin' wasstill graduallyleaving the mightyhead, red, but not forgreener pastures but forwhiterones ... so the quantumleap from Leap, from the landof the long barrenground to the landof the longwhitecloud took place and twomore fitzgeralds with mouthstofeed arrived in N.Z. around 1852 howabout you ... but they are even more on the sideof correctness when they are standingtogether at ther samegate dont ya tinkso there Patrick Mika, ai I do will yahave anotherpaddy, Oh ai 1 will tanksvery much ... the eviction of the ancestor whonow wandered lonelyin thecrowd withonly the company of hisbabe and the sorrow of his deadcolleen haunting him accrossthe barren land as the bansheehowls andhe tries to sleepin the nightly bogholes dugdaily and coveredby the turf, and with regret he hadfin allyto con cede that he couldnot find Gadiva's gate in reality ...

Here Joe Blogs writes his own personal views in Joe's Blog:
I want somebody to know, for she might say someting tonight at your meeting. The bagpacker (Oh, come my dear Franz, just one more dance) has over 4oo bugs from me! In January I stayed more than 10 days there and that room had been my 'pensive citadel.' So it is: 10 days x 25, that is 250, - at least then they make me pay 50 bugs for their little batch - there was nothing else. And I was so nice so change for another girl into there, who didn't had a place - but it was my birthday, and I had stomach cramps - what some woman have every 4 weeks – the trial, at least one night I stayed in there - so 25, plus 50 = 300 bugs. Then I stayed now, after Easter there for three days:
Of Atlantean shoulders, fit to bear
The weight of mightiest monarchies
- luckily Lovele Rosali was there, the sister from Uncle Jacob, or as Richmal William Crompton said of The Beatles in 1964 'I simply can't understand the effect they have on the young. I suspect that one contributing element is the tom-tom rhythm of the music (?) that arouses a sort of primitive frenzy in the hearers. I suppose that the savage is quite near the surface of civilization! I've listened to them and tried to understand but feel only fury and horror. One can only hope the craze will be short-lived!'
That's it for now, yours, Joe.

... in the rushto killat Kilrush William Butler notyet Yeats nyet wrote and I quoteofa tumbling hesaw with twelveyearold eyes ... atumblingdice of the tippswho would laterappear in the centralotago fieldof goldin competition withthe Chinese butthats another story as you will findout, Jen knows when for they built the Otago rail also, ah so ... Thesherrif, a strongforce ofpolice and aboveall the crowbarbrigade, a body composedof the lowest andmost debauchedruffians werepresent who watch snow fall until it covers thirty three buildings, then KAPOW ... at a signalfrom the sherrif the miserable inmatesof thecabins were draggedout, thatchedroofs were torndown, earthenwalls battered inby crow bars (where crows hangout or perhaps the 'Palais de Glace', even), screamingwomen, the affectionate childhood thumping and bumping of halfnakedchildren, paralysedgrandmother and totteringgrand da were hauledout, andso it waswith the Patrickte arikirubezahlalexisfitzgerald who nowheaded for whatheknewnot, butwhichwouldbe Aotearoa ... One dream S.M.H. had as shelay with Sister Joyce with love as their medication that eve ning butit took her entirely away sothat when Joyce's Sister awoke in the morning expectingto find her lover she was no longer there andshe neversaw her again ... Himself somewhat taken abackin time and place butnow restored to manhood wherewas he now, didhe workupon the railway, didhe ridthe streets of grime, without the headof, must be headingoff now, the great white mass ofan anglican party wasin half-swing, protesting ants, cat a holicks spilling drinkon the fair dinkum richwhite car pet, poodlestrudel, nolight flickering onoroff, nobright ideas only the steady dullduty bound lives of the flock, no flocknocker except for sleeping, no tortured souls no laughing no weeping, godhelps those that help themselves so helpyourselves and to hell with the rest, no rest for the wicked, I'm so tired, I haven't slept awank a ship of light sailsby in the darkness, metaphor omo metaphor it's realenough and Himself has taken ona seriarse ness which belies his out wardgoingnature, where is henow, heknows but wont let thecat out of thebag despite the inter minableisland ferrymeowing shutup, boot! He dreams he wasa nun, flying zip undone, as grandiose as an 'archeopteryx' and he dreams he wasa snow man that noman should tear Unbebagen, lying bleeding on loves' stoneywhite ground and send snow sounds to a person you like, but now the dreamis over, what can say, the bubblesburst of love again no romantic beauty inner orouter, just stones and facts, survival tactics not evena did you know?

However, Fred dismissed this as one of Alex's 'Munchausen Moments' and Bruno interloped in agreement, saying that 'such a notion is childish and narcissistic, and completely contrary to what Fred had in mind.' Alex laughed it off, retorting with 'Ora howa bout this!' and explaining further that it was Mid-Lent when one goes without a hat. 'Lunch time,' said Fred, and Alex stopped his ancestral journey to eat his kai, which smelled delicious through his nose-pod. Bruno arrived not long after to relieve Fred and bring Alex his afternoon pills, so he could resume his ancestral dreamtime.

... workether, ethics of dollarbill birds, queensface smearedsmirkinglike filth, here comes the Smir King major itty, no titty, not the Filthy Few factsand figures Irish population (due entirely to copulation in the firsinst) of Otago shotup, indeed Shotover 3,154 (eleven p.c) from 206, 1861, and then in Cromwell, nay Lowbum, O'Brien wasshooting at those who went buy elswhere, I'll take you homea gain Kathleen, no youwont be causeshe's dead, but has risena gain oursister welcome as prophesised in the holy youknowwhat, where did you get that what, but the houris getting late and the child, I mean trial is a bout to begin beit gin orbit of whiskey be gin the child, 1 mean trial of Archbishop Listen, now hear this, for treason trees are green, Teresa after the Easter Proclamation came one of many childs from everywhere, HEC, I mean trials from out of the Roisin Dub, from the dark just after the Shoneen, butfrom inside the Rosaleen, herself as opposed to himself united but still fighting in Himself, from between the sheets on the occasion and make different sounds by hitting different parts of it ... Twopenny O'Reagan and Conlan himself defended at the child of Bishop Liston, not yetarched and I mean trial, SS means all my trials, Lord, soon be October, the month of Our Lady ... Patrick Fitzgerald stepped down off the planeat Mangere Air Port tired and still ... thus calledbe cause when asked by hispoorer clients howmuch he wouldcharge to defend them would invariably reply 'Oh, notmuchmore than twopence I cant imagine,' started his intro into his defencecouncil summing up withnot the customary 'May itplease yourhonour, Mr Foreman and gentle menof the jury etc,' but with the more unauthordox, seditious even, phrase 'What the fook is Patrick Fitzgerald doing here, stepping down off a plane which hasn't been invented at an airport which hasn't even been fooking builtyet!' 'Order! Order!' cried the Stringing judge and immediately awaiter appeared witha pencil and notepad. However, 'His Magesty of the Ego', Mr Conlan, whispered something into Mr O'Reagan's ear, who then muttered 'Mmmnmmmn, 1 see,' and the judge seeing that things were atiast inorder, dismissed the waiter and said, 'You may proceed Mr O'Reagan.' ... trying toget usedtohis newname. My name is James O'Donnell, he kept repeating to himself (is it himself?) in his own mind ... the section of the Crimes Act under which the Bishop is indicted is declatory of the common law. The Crown Prosecutor has already indicated that here-lieson the twosub sections, U2, withor without you too section 118 and whiskey on Sundays!

At this juncture an unsolicited e-mail from Ancestry.com appeared ...
Our   Name   in   History   is   the   story   of   your   last   name.
What does your family name mean and where does it come from? When and how did people sharing your name immigrate to the U.S.? What did they do and how did they live? Our Name in History is a great way to spend time with mom and learn about the history that brought your family together ... but do not explain about the powder to the friends to whom you send.

Also in his own mind he keptre peating the image of the young Britishsoldier he had killednot aweek before, It had takenone thousandy ears of English oppression, allthe storiesfrom the oldones ... which made it seditious touse words ... told with the terrorof brutal reality being relived of the Blackand Tandays, all the horror of the re cent troubles since 1969 ... calculated to raisedis content or dis affection among Newzealand citizens, orto pro mote illwill and hostil itybe tween ... all the memories of the maimed and murdered friends and family dealt to by these Brittish guardians of liberty it had taken all these things Russian through hismind like a streamofsky suddenly swollen anddang erous from flooding emotion ... different classes of citizen. The real question is what did the Bishop intend? Of course, toa large ex tent, his intention is tobe gathered from the lanuage he used (English, sohis intention was obviously questionable) but ... toget Patrick Fitzgerald to pull the triggeron this young english soldierboy. Notlong (the palandrome for notlob would be bolton) before, this soldier had been an arrogant, self-assured memb er of the best trained street armyin the world, meteringout British Justice to the savage, uncivilised Irish ... in its verynature the definition of sedition is vague. Thus it becomes afact, a question offact, and hence one solefor the jury, after red herring counsel's addresses at the bar (and telephone numbers as the Bishop said to the actress) and sub jectto the ass istance of Honour's review of the law and evidence ... Now he was more like a squealing pig (is a pigsarse still porkdoctor dean? Here Fred's interest in JL eon ardo, Oct 9, 1898, JL's B'Day, mendips at menlove, more famous than JC, no love-affair is recorded! Alex denies ALL knowledge of carnality with BE, then now-) writhing and pleading for mercy. Then, MaD's flirtation with illustrated papers over as it was considered 'most inappropriate', as there was nomore arguing. 'You showed my people no mercy,' Fitzgerald said quietly and pulled the trigger, the grimace characteristic of smiling, which twists up the corners of the mouth like an infant at the breast when it is satisfied and satiated imagines one thousand suns in the sky at the same time ... Of course when the language is so plain that it speaks for itself the duty of the jury is mucheasier and shoulda persona directly incite others to violence or crime of anykind they will notbe allowed toplead the innocence of their motive or the goodness of their object, or to vary the plain meaning of their language ... 'Mr James O'Donnell,' the customs officer looked at him, wanting a response. Pat rick lookedat the uniform and fora ninstance had for gotten his newidentity. Hewas justa bout tosay Fitzgerald whichwas hisown name which hisown mother hadgiven him at childbirth in a Tutu ... Here ofcourse the case isnotso serious, butit will doubt lessbea greed that the language employed, asex plained in the evidence evidently is very differ entfromthat which appear edin the Pressre ports of the Bish opspeach ... 'Oh, yes, I'm sorry. Sure I'm james O'Donnell bit tired youknow itsa longa longalong flight from London and yougetta fewof the drinks downyou on the way, ha!' ... you will agree with me having regard to the highoff ice of the Bishop, his frankness (no letmebe Frank, youwere him last night!) in the witness-box, and his satisfactory (isn't that the place where thy make satis, now Patrick Mika) mannerin which heex plained the meaning of his speech ... 'Have you anything to declare, Mr O'Donnell?' 'Only megenious in the traditionof meancestors!' The official offal blackbottle waved himon in amanner which said typical bloodymad Irish, 'Next!' Sweet Saint Patrick, thatwas close, Patrickmuttered to himself (again what was himself doing there when he should have been attending to the child, I mean trial of Bishop - of the 1920s - Liston this man himself was beginning to take on certain characteristics ofthe man Himself, frightening in its enormity!) as he made his wayout of the customs area to collect hisbags and lookfor the person hewas tomeet ... not merely that hehadno malicious in tent, or anyother unfixed abode, but that hehad been the victim of much unnecesssary and coarse criticism and that the indictment canin no way be sustained (in Norway?) In connection with the speech, Gentlemen, sleep two walls away from each other for it isnot anti cipatedthat youwill necessarily agree with all the views therein expressed, for the word *nibio* was mis-translated as 'vulture', thus the whole argument by Fred as put to Alex and Bruno regarding the Egyptian goddess R. Mutt falls to the ground, but I digress ... ashe lookeda round the concourse (brothers) the first thing that struck himwas the numberof darkskinned people. It wasa real surprise for him (a real surprise for himyummmmnunm!) for the onlything he really knew a bout N.Z. was that it wasa country which strove tobe more English than the English ... everyone is entitled to their opinions on the questionof the day and in this respectone citizen isas good asanother, to the last woman standing. Moveover, what doyou mean I mean moreover, they are entitledto persuade othersto share their views on as I shallshow presently shellshock, thereis nolimit in this respect save that theymay notemploy improper language, norad vocate violins to attain their end, if there's music in hell it will beplayedon bagpipes, Jimmy Wild said that ... the iron icnature of this amused him and he was laughing to himself (whoelse?) about how the peoplehe camefrom were known as the Black Irish not to mention the Puck himself (also) when his thoughts were interrupted byaman saying 'Hey bro, are you James O'Donnell?' ...

Here Joe Blogs writes his own personal views in Joe's Blog:
SHE would not say anything negative about me, if that can be her older daughter, help me Rhonda. or her husbund, Domimik. Her younger daughter, Claire and her family likes me a lot too, like florie does ... only Rhonda ... - but, hey she didn't want any money! I stayed there a bit longer than a week, what we said, for I wasn't feeling well. The only thing I need, for I am very exhausted, would be sleep, writing (bookauthors do that on the road to Rameses) and reading. I got sick after one week - but I WANTED to leave last Tuesday - that would have been 2 1/2 weeks. But, SHE said: no, but if you don't have a place shure, you can stay longer - and I said, no I'll leave, for you want me out of the house! Within the very ears of insulted authority, I could not myself forebear joining in it: subdued to this, not so much by the unhappy *étourderie* of the trunk, as the effect it had on the Seven Sleepers ... further to my **previous blog** concerning Richmal Crompton and The Beatles I note that in a collection of short stories titled *William and the Pop Singers* she is not adversed to 'making capital' out of the very band she so despises! Just listen to this:
'Douglas slipped the strap over his head and began to beat on it with his sticks.
His voice rose, nasal and strident, over the beats of the drum.
'Moon girl, my moon girl,
I'm comin' to you soon, girl,
Shootin' up the moonbeams
'Cos I'm in love with you'
The other three were swinging and writhing their bodies in time to the rhythm.
'Yeah! Yeah! Yeah!' yelled Ted.
'Up the silvery beams, girl
 Where I seen you in my dreams, girl
Dream girl, dream girl
I'm in love with you'
 'Yeah! Yeah! Yeah!'
'It's a winner, boys!' shouted Chris exultantly, throwing the drum on the ground.
'It's a winner!'
'It'll need a bit of fixing,' said Ted, 'but it's a winner all right. And-Chris, boy, you're not wasting your life. You're bringing joy to youth, and youth to old age. You're bringin' joy an' hope an' youth to a weary world.'
Yeah! Yeah! Yeah! Yelled Pete.'
- that's the sea of illusion in which the young were drowning and, indeed pop culture was the *mal la mer* of youth in 1965 according to William's creator: more next time:
That's it for now, yours, Joe.

now, having heard the evidence after the eveningdance I askew to dismiss from your minds asfaras possible the aspersions castupon the Bishopby the Press andby various public bodies and to judge him onlyon what you have heard in this court. Not only have the witnesses for the Crown been serverely shaken in cross-examination but severalof them have admitted that the Bis hop, when dealing (hop) with the Easter uprising and subsequent events, stated that hewas treading water, reading from alist andeven they weresat isfied that when his Lordship spoke about the 155 men and women, three of whom were priests (but we'll neverknow which, nun but Himself knows and he's in the Purification Phamber Piece where a 'Munchausen Moment' may occur for a person who claims to suffer from complexity of mind or schizophrenia, I've got a funny feeling, if we remove the ceiling said Fred, meaning the sealant we all put around our psyche, and a kite, like a vulture, is a bird!) who during and since 1916 had diedfor Ireland, hewas not referring only to those who who were killed in the Rising, but also those who who were conceived and born because of the 'rising' ... unsettled and stunned he answered 'Yes.' As he collected himself (where did he collect himself from?) and hisluggage together he looked at the tall, well-built Mäori man whohad greeted him. His thoughts were wild but he said, 'How doyou knowmyname, did you look up de number? I was supposed to meet some one called Paddy O'Connell.' 'Yeah, that's me,' the man smiled and gave Fitzgerald an unfamiliar street-wise handshake. They both walked silently towards the bar andit was only when they both hada pint of beer before them that O'Donnell felt relax edenough to speak to O'Connell ... and thathe referred to the Black and Tansalone, not justas a mixture of beerandstout, but as also murderers foremost. Even asit stands the speech unex plained by evidence cannotbe reason ablysaid tobea damaging inferences which the Crown (the Brattish Croam, as van the seated man wearing a top hat might say) seeks to draw therefrom. Taking the first para graph onwhich witch the Crown relies hislord ship, any thing goes in, anything goes out the snake winds around bothhere and about, early in the speech referred the numbers of Irish people whohad beendriven from their homes because their foreign masters didnot want the landpeopled by Irish menandwomen but preferredto makeit a cattleranch for the snobsof the empire, the Irish umpire raised his finger in the air indicating notout ... 'Andyou know aboutme then now, do you Paddy?' Fitzgerald asked halfchallenging hishost and halfhoping that hewas surelya mong friends. 'Oh, yeah,' answered Paddydrinking, Paddy, Drink King, his beer with a great relish, not in a pickle, 'But I think the least said the bet tera round here, e?' By the time they left the air port, brandy, whiskey, gin (thatswhat did me in) both men had drunkand talked enough to be completly re laxed in each other's company. They strode out towards the car park, where the cars play calling Mr Carswell, tap this well and we're away, red Fred Adair singing bringing in the reins and shouting at the tops of their voices twentyfourhours from Tulsa, they were happy ... here the Bishop wasal luding to an historical fact, an his tooori caal fa aaaaa act, a deplorable fact, a de ploooor ableee faa aa a ct, you will remembergentlemen, that hewas speaking to an Irish audience on a subject which the Irish heart beat feels deeply, *prit son fils et la meme,* [six words underlined in green] oh, what can it mean? It maybe diffi cult foryou who are not Irish to under stand that feeling. But as the Lybian writer of yore, and yours! Sheik el a Bar, says 'He jests at scars, that never felt a wound' ... Paddy's car, SERIAL NO. #9,331, wasan oldbeat up Mark II Zephyr known in the suburbs as a 'Laundry Barge' which rode like its namesake the west wind haiku ...

Zephyr, west wind, to you
A poem was written
This is mine Mark 2

... and Patrick noticed how differentit looked to the other cars belonging to the moreaffluent air portpatrons, the BMWs, Mercedes, and myriads of latemodel Japanese cars. 'They'll never suspectus in this Paddy, they think the IRA are all millionaires from Lybia.' O'Connelllauugh andswung the carinto the mainroad towards the motorway ... I trust, however, you possess sufficient of the dramatic instinct toput yours elves in our place, O'Reagan continued (whilst smiling ironically to himself, who in turn smiled back as if to say thatsa bit below the belt 2d, accusing the English of dramaticin stinct) for I am proud to be of Irish ex tractionmy self, and not to make false a, near the beach of Tusitala llowance for Llewellyn whenhe comes running but to feel some sympathy for the sentiment of deep indig nation ... Patrick was struck by two (more later) main things as the car roared along towards Auckland City. The first was the light, the quality of brilliance and sharpness in the sky and secondly he hadn't expect Deaf Ted Auckland tobe sobig and modern. The craic was good be tween the two as the car rattled and hummed a long the motorway through the *Horapollo* passage. Patrick said to Paddy 'Have many of the Maoris got the Irish names like yourself now?' 'Ah, yeah bro! We got alot in common, e! Here,' he said handing Fitzgerald a bottle of beer, (let a vine grow, water every day) 'I'd rather have a bottleinfrontofme than a frontalabottomy he he he, ai! But apart from the fact that my greatgreatgreat grandfather hada bit ofa liking for the duskymaidens whohid him when he wason the run for deserting during the landwars, there is quite a lot of overlaps between our two cultures' ... with which they'd recall the evictions which drove such immense numbersof Irishpeople from their country and which accounts in no smallmeasure for the abiding affection rnanyof their descendants still cherish, is the word association footfall softly, softly, for the landofsky their ancestors who suffered such cruel and in excusable wrongs ... Patrick drank and listened as Paddy parallelled the two races, Galway and Wingatui, their love of fighting and their love of art, their strong oral tradition and love of words, their poetic legends and mythologies, their dying and sexual cravings that paralleled the opposititional qualities attributed to the Leonardoesque smile of the Homo Lisa, men have made you ... mylearned friend invites you to take seriously the paragraph in which the Bishop states that Erin has not got all she asked for, not all that her sons and daughters died for, no, not even Clémence the Unfauved, but that she had secured an in stalment of her free domand was determined to have the whole, til death duty parts ... here Patrick began to laugh. 'What's funny?' asked Paddy ... the vast majority of Irish people share the feeling and it is absurd to suggest that the views expressed by Bishop Liston are anything other than that which any citizen is entitled (and indeed should O'Reagan thought to himself, who concurred) ... 'I've gota friend in Dublin who fancies himself a bit of a poet, and his Egyptian dream-bird can sing' said Fitzgerald, 'Brendan that's his name, now he wrote a poem once about a friend of ours called the Ballad of Ryan O'Corky.' 'Lets hear it, bro,' said Paddy and Patrickre cites thus:

His skin was bumpy, palid and chalky
Yet this never held him back
For he was ethnic without being black

... at this theyboth cracked-up laughing ... the commendation of Mr de Valera as the manwho has carried Ire land thus far and who wouldsee that the leadersof Irelandwere not duped by England is also wellwithin the boundsof freespeech, a freebee for a bone, so they cut up a painting and let them be lost in the wind ... 'Ha, thats real funny about being ethnic without being black. I remember readinga book when I was last inside by Robert Graves, e, where he said one of the things which blew the Englishaway when they camehere was the similarity be tween the Mäori tribal setupand the old Irish wayof doing things, the tohanga, the whole bit. That probably made them even more determined to undermine Maoritanga, ai' ... though the passage would certainly have been less liable to mis interpretation, more especially as thereis criticism this country iseagerto mis interpret, had the Bi shop make itplain that he ref erred to the Government and not the peopleof en gland ... travelling along Tamaki Drive towards Öräkei bothmen wentsilent enjoying the beauty of the trees, thesky, the water. The car turned into Watene Crescent. 'Come on bro, haere mai, welcome to home.' ... His Irish audience under stood what he meant by saying it was a means of getting away from nature – 'another dream of what art is about, indeed they have too many historical reasons for doingso, so they cut a hole in a bag filled with seeds of any kind and placed the bag where there is wind, that is a windbag! ... Patrick looked at the statehouse where he would beliving andas hewas surrounedbya sea of brown smilingfaces asall the childrenin the neighbour hood collectedex citedly hewas thinkingof hisown home asmall councilhouseinthe south of Ireland, the O'Bremen 'peat-bog corpses' for egg ... I referto that of the pressreport which has givenrise to the stron gestde nun ciation. I concede atonce that the in dictment would befully just ified if the Bishop reallyspoke as the pressreports him. Assuredly, how ever, he has abundantly satisfied you ... James had been introducedto the family. Also, the Auckland Sinn Fein man came tosee him to give him money and tell him a bout the lie of the land. 'You'll be layin' low fora bit, and then wewant a few things done.' 'What's that now Danny?' ... that he did not apply the word 'murdered' in connection with those who were killed inaction in 1916, and that he only used the term in connection with the Blackandtans during 1921 ... 'Well, Patrick we know there are U.D.R. men herin New Zealand wholike yourself are on the run and have been given new identities. Unlike yourself these boysare here with the complicity of the British Government and possibly the New Zealand Government is involved inan even more active way than just turning ablindeye' ... here let me state that we cannot recede from our contention that the men and women of the blackandtans were murderers ... 'So it was formore than just the humanitarians that you got me out here.' Daniel O'Brien looked at this young killer and all the feelings for the land he wasof but had never been to came upon him. For a moment Patrick became O'Brien's own ancestor standing before him, his grand father driven into escape and exile for being a murderous Fenian bastard, an Irish savage, for fighting to regain his country from the English rulers ... the plain people of Ireland, indeed the people of the Irish race everywhere, hold in reverence the menandwomen whohave foughtand bled for the cause of nationality ... O'Brien said 'the Mäori people in New Zealand notonly have a similar outlook and culture to our own but their struggle to be who they are in their own country is also the same, and it is basically against the same system and people ... just as they revere Robert Emmet, who engaged in a forlorn hope, they cherish the memories of those who died in 1916' ... this concurred with the fantasy of father-murder, especially significant to the young according to the head of Medusa, although don't ask me why, or what goes on in your heart!

At this juncture an unsolicited e-mail from Ancestry.com appeared ...
Our Name in History is the story of your last name.
What does your family name mean and where does it come from? When and how did people sharing your name immigrate to the U.S.? What did they do and how did they live? Our Name in History is a great way to spend time with mom and learn about the history that brought your family together ... and in Fred's Faustian restlessness he nearly had Alex burn the paper! Well, there was a nude in a bathtub and another nude wearing black stockings!!!

'Is there any IRA type Movement that the Mäori people fight under?' 'In the past there were many rebel groups who opposed British rule and the Treaty of Waitangi but they got heavily stamped on especially when the settlers arrived to claim 'their land' which had been promised to them' ... may I remind you finally, thatone of the men involved in the Easter Rising was Patrick Mika Collins whowas sub sequently Commander-in-Chief of the Irish Republican Army but who is now a minister of the crown aman who the peopleof both countries feeland hope will domuch to reconcile the two nations ... your jobis to breakinto the UDR exile scheme and expose it, we've actually got a lead onone of them who lives herein the Eastern Suburbsof Auckland who we think you willbeable to identify ... bear in mind thatin everyage and everycountry history records acts of heroism which were illegal and atleast as faras the chiefact ors were concerned, futile and disastrous ... Patrick Fitzgerald fell asleep almost immediately anditwas the firstime ina week that whenhe closed hiseyes he didnot see the eyesof his victim looking at him in terror ... I am convinced, having regardto hishigh office, the fact that hisco-religionists are a small minority in this country and the impotence of being frank (and earnest) and ready mannerin which he has demeaned him selfin the wit nessbox, that you willagree the Bishop and the actress cannot lightly be presumed to have intended sedition ... cruising along Kepa Rd., the reggaebeat pounding them towards the Glen Innes pub. Wakeup tomorrow with the G.I. blues e, bro, said Rewi. I reckon Rangireplied and theyall laughed ... remember that within the limits I havequoted everycitizen is legallyfree to express whatever opinion they please ... as soonas they walked through the door O'Donnell gota fix on him. He hadnt seenhim forfive years but Patrick would haveknown him blindfolded as indeed hehad when William Craig, Sergeant in the UDR had taken him in for questioning about anarms ship ment meant for the IRA theyhad held him for forty hours with a hoodover his head and no food ... but these are politicalquestions andyou donot need telling that politicalquestions areoft sandwitched with the fiercest passion ... he had raised

Craig's ire bymerely suggesting that itwas the UDR whowere the real terrorists in Ireland the fact that theygot their weapons supplied freeby the English didn't make them more moral, only legal under Brittish law ... those who profess unpopular opinions or principles not properly under stood areoft exposed to unfair attack by opponents whomakea cheap parade of loyalty to the established orderof thingsby levelling lying accusations of dis loyalty or dat loyalty hey sorry you aint the child of Bishop Liston is you, you mean trial, man, oh yeah! And sedition against brave and upright citizens, i.e., pants, jacket, shirt, stockings, 3 MaD frenchies - Dr Ferdinand Tribout, Chauvel, Dr R. Dumouchel, alligarters, wild boats, garriffes, lepers, and Uncle Tom Cobra and all, Holy Moses and his frozen Michelangelo wrath in his pain mingled with contempt and all, etc ... he went and called Paddy and told him what wasup I wasn't expecting this despite O'Brien's briefing, anyway you'd better get overhere, overthere, overhere, and Paddy, come prepared. He went back to the bar and told the others he was just going to get a bit of freshair, he didnt want to lose Craig ... 'Wehaveno King but Caesar' shouted the Scribes and Pharisees of Jerusalem longago was sofar togo, sofaa soifua, and againsaid theyto the Sky-Pilot, punch us, 'If thou release Himself thou art not Caesar's friend.' Yet they hated Caesar andall that his Governmentmeant. They affected loyalty to Caesar because they desired to have Himself declared guilty whom they accused of stirring up sedition ... suddenly he was grabbed around the throat and he felt a pistol stuck into his back. 'So its James O'Donnell is it, aye! The Irish werealways a bloody literary lot of lunatics, right Jimmy. But we know who you murdering Papists are killing young Brittish soldiers nowarewe, ha!' Craig held thegun to Fitzgerald's head ... itis not without reason that a distinguised historian has said thatno legal process hasbeen more shamelessly perverted to tyranical andun just ends than that of treason and sedition ... Craig cocked the pistol and with his finger on the trigger, said 'the world wont miss the death of another' and a shot rangout. Patrick looked around in wonder that hewas still alive. He thought he had been shot but Paddy grabbed himby the arm, 'Lets get out of here, bro! Here catch!' Fitzgerald caught the rifle as they both got in the Mark 11 and spedoff into the night ... Dr Liston really said nothing which he orany other citizen hadnot a perfect right to say, to wit, 'Great is the Diana of the Ephesians', but by publishing a garbled condensation ofhis speech, servedup under misleading headlines and criticising its own version the press inflamed the publicmind to an extent that would have been impossible were it not for the fact that the speaker was a Catholic Bishop and was seated next to the artist's father who was seated next to the 'seated nude' during a chess game ... the next morninga report appeared in the paper headed GANG KILLING, Aman by the name Sammy Cordon believed tobea member of a white supremicist gang, was shot dead outside the Glen Innes Tavern last night, where they hang a bottle behind a canvas. Police said two men, believed to be Mäori or Polynesian, were seen leaving the hotel in a Zephyr car which was later found abondoned in Tautari St, Öräkei, Police also said they were looking fora .22 rifle, no other weapon was involved ...

At this juncture an unsolicited e-mail from Ancestry.com appeared ...
Our   Name   in   History   is   the   story   of   your   last   name.
What does your family name mean and where does it come from? When and how did people sharing your name immigrate to the U.S.? What did they do and

how did they live? Our Name in History is a great way to spend time with mom and learn about the history that brought your family together ...

Fred and Bruno were discussing their charge PMF, aka Mad Alex, *Moses and Monotheism* watching his REMS as he slept, having heard the Bishop's evidence and his trans parent (you see I told you there was a child and that the Bishop was a parent doesn't matter howit happened trans or other wise virgins its always been apparent) confidence toyou tofind a verdict truthfulness and accordingly I appeal with Not Guilty ... which was the judge meant and so it was and as Conlan and O'Reagan went off to gether in opposite directions him self stood looking, watching and waiting for his wife not hiswife andas they embraced his head was full of skull ... a great sadness swept overhim, overtime, all down the days he realised no matter howmany lives he lead how many incarnations how many carnal dreams or spiritual thoughtshow old they lived to be, how close they came to ... their love could not be of this world and he wept silent and inwardly for he knew that even if he lived to be a thousand year reich ora million dollar rich that he had met the woman he loved, which is more than a lot of people do, but that they could never be of this world ... *Quando para mucho mi amore de felice, corazon, Mundo paparazzi mi amore chicka ferdy, para sol, Cuesto obrigado tanta mucho que* can eat it, *carousel* ... a great storm blew up and the sky darkened and her image also darkened but he knew she would always return with each flash of lightning, with each roll of thunder and then the rains would beat heavily completely engulfing the headland and he never felt more alone ... c1920 the head or rather the skull of becket into which they, deBal et al, drill a small, almost invisible, hole in the centre of the canvas and see the room through it, would not have been as well formed as it would come to be so, that when himself first discovered it it was more likely full of crecket or silent movies and after the trial of the child of Mrs Liston had been witnessed he picked up the empty skull holding it out stretched in one hand proclaiming alas poor sam we will know him well but at this stage we are still waiting for not I butyou andyour Nana in a green blouse ... are a simpleton ... but he loved the flight of the hawk and could distinguish it from all others, no wonder he called himself a conquistador. He would stand rapt, gazing at the long preenings, the quivering poise, the wings lifted for the plummet drop the wild reascend, fascinated by such extremes of need, of pride, of patience and solitude himself turned almost automatically from his wifeless reveries into a hawk and with quick glance overhis shoulder at what mighthave been he flew soaring southwards in the past ... 'you know the trouble with Fred is' Bruno was saying to Magic Alex, who had woken up for his afternoon tea and his cricket fix, 'that Fred is too hasty to interpret people's dreams. And you don't get nowhere if yer too hasty, do yer, yer gotta, gotta, gotta, gotta, gotta tread softly, let them rise slowly like the yeast of dreams. Otherwise it just ain't fair ...'

But Fred could see that Magic was about to take on one of his multiple personalities. He was turning into the PSM, which always led him to feel like he was about to lose control of his or his temper, his reason or his mind. It was also called nervous anxiety, the kind that engaged Fred the most: that which he enjoyed best about psychiatric nursing. In that sence he was not unlike Murphy, although he had never gone off his rocker himself. When the ego got caught and threatened by the clash of forces between the superego and the id, it would first struggle to deal with it. When the anxiety became too much for Alex he just became something or someone else, and usually led to a situation where there was a conflict between freedom and responcibility …

A jpg image arrived at this point
the clicket team of the century nineteen is seen on the screen of the individual eye-pod alex. Byronic columns arise through bat-infested wooded backdrops, and withered Mordor and unhealthy Heccate moves towards Magic's latest design like a ghost. The man stands off-centre stage right, aloof and judgemental in his Old School Tie and sporty sports jacket. Turn left at Greenland and see The Ice-man who from cometh from Iceland, Gandar Thor Cortes yodelling up the canyon, with the ice-pick that killed Trotsky held on high, while the woman, Nella Fantasia, is twisting something about in her hand as though she was making *Knodel* or dumplings, in long flowing skirts and chastity-belt blouse, she holds her hands to her forehead, a nude standing stage left, as though she is in Esseee-anguish. Above hovers the three Children of the Apocalypse, riding towards Valhalla in their little bright green pleasure machine – they, like their parents, are travelling light across the university into the 'out of it' unknown, while the nude with brown skin, the girl now knowing she was about to meet her tipuna, Te Rauparaha, said put your shadows together until they become one …

A DVD is now showing: of a cricket match set in Auckland in the 1970's and all that as the train pulled out of Morningside Station and swung in a curve to the left in a steady climb towards Kingsland he felt a surge of subdued excitement and illicit pleasure. It was the first illegitimate day that he had taken off work and he remembered, as though drawn in ink and gouache, with guilt and sheer joy my wife's voice lying over the telephone as she told my boss that I would not be into the office that day because I had put my back out on the weekend whilst lifting some posts for a fence I was building around our home in New Lynn. It had taken a lot of persuasion and argument the night before to get her to do what she called 'This immoral act'. I had worked at this government department for nearly ten years, since Maureen and I were first married and had settled down along with the dust, and had never taken a day off. 'And all for a bloody game of cricket!' she had screamed in outrage and incomprehension as she envisaged the whole of our safe, secure suburban fortress crumbling into a degenerate void. 'Don't shout, dear, you'll wake the children. It's only one day and …' 'Don't you, don't wake the children, me! It's more than 'only one day' and you know it.' In the middle of this husband and wife moment Alex the fish had a 'Munchausen Moment' of some significance, for it was forty years ago today that Sargent Pepper unleashed the dogs of PEACE, while Gigantor Garguntua sat astride Notre Dame and turned his stream of urine on Paris, with everybody shouting 'WHICH SIDE ARE YOU ON!!!' Unfortunately, only the dogs could hear the whistle blowing, and then only after being released from an extended chord at the end of a day in a dog's life. Imagine (sic) how different the world might be if we had all heard that 'lost' chord. And now its back to time for tea and meet the wife … 'This little escapade threatens everything we've worked for and believed in. I thought after ten years you might have changed bit now I see … now I see … Oh! What's the use! Neither of us could say any more that evening but I knew she would do what I wanted. So the next morning I woke not to the usual sound of the 6.30 alarm but to my oldest son and daughter coming in and kissing me goodbye before they left for school. 'How come dad's not goin' to work' I heard Jenny say and Maureen answer, 'Well, your father's not well.' Then she came into our room, the baby in one arm and my breakfast begrudgingly balancing in her free hand. 'There!' she said, 'And I hope ya choke on it!' But as he walked out of the door I heard a stifled chuckle coming from her, and as I watched her back disappear she suddenly became again the beautiful young woman who had something in the way she moved when I had met at the St Patrick's Day dance all those years ago.

He stepped down off the train onto what passes for a platform at Kingsland Station. As the old carriages of the City Rail train moved on up towards Mt Eden he had his usual feeling of living in a world which no longer existed. For every day of the last decade when he caught the 7.30 a.m. train from New Lynn and then the 5.15 p.m. home from Auckland, he was aware that he travelled on a transport system which had been condemned to death several times over, *Fluctuat nec mergitur*. As he, Patrick Malone (the PSM), walked past the Shamrock Rest Home towards Eden Park, he reflected upon the metaphoric elements which led him to go out of his way each of these work days in order to catch the train.

It was true the bus would be cheaper and quicker and he would have been able to leave his little nest a bit later. He concluded, however, that these were the very reasons he did not follow such logic, 'throw it off a high building' he thought, as he always did in the face of incomprehension. It must be an assertion of individuality, a Celtic perverseness against a puritanical system which ensnared his life in so many ways. By catching the train he could, in his own way, make his mark against the English barbarians as if were he in Ireland he might join the Republican Army!

'Ten dollars, please sir.' Patrick handed over the blue money and walked through the gates to freedom. Yes, that was the only word to describe the feeling he got from being enclosed behind fences in the midst of a multitude of people all assembled together to experience the magic of a game of cricket. He walked around until he found a programme which he purchased along with a hot pie and a can of Coca Cola, then he found a place to settle for the rest of the day. Patrick had brought with himself a small transistor radio for he enjoyed nothing more than the excitement which came from the commentary box. All the wonderful terms, the vast knowledge of the game and the witty talk from visiting commentators are intertwined in a matrix and conspired in him to make him imagine that this must be what heaven was like, that is, place canvas A on canvas B and hang them together, while 'waiting at the lights, know what I mean?'

Patrick Malone sat alone amidst the steadily building crowd. He was entranced at the variety of people around him, and like a blind person whose eyes are opened after several years being aware of darkness, he looked and looked and looked. Eventually his curiosity of events around him diminished and his attention focussed on the programme which held all the details of the game itself.

A DVD is now showing: of a cricket match set in Auckland in the 1970's

The two teams for this one day international game had never met before and whilst the New Zealand team was a familiar sight to the Eden Park ground, the Invitation Out of It Eleven were wholly new to this part of the world. Some individual names, such as James K. Baxter and Te Rauparaha, her tipuna and the Out of It Captain, were known locally, but in the main, whilst people may have heard of individual personalities at various times, they certainly were not known here in the South Pacific as international cricketers. But Patrick Malone was spell-bound as he read over and over the names of his various heroes. He, of course, had followed each of their careers on and off the twenty-two yard pitch and unlike most of the Auckland crowd, he supported them against the 'straight' New Zealand eleven.

All these years he had been doing all the right things. He was married, had children, a mortgage, was paying off a new car which his wife Maureen used because he refused to drive. It was his love of public transport and his passion for cricket which Patrick Malone had cherished as his only expression of individuality and rebellion. However, these feelings and thoughts were far from straightforward, and can only be described as an excursion into the pseudo-hieratic style of Deraingement, in MaD Munchausenian terms.

In the days when he himself had been 'out of it' he had detested cricket as the ultimate experience of the straight, elitist, middle-class whom he had despised. But he had detected a certain elitism also amongst his fellow revolutionaries and anarchists which irked him. So, as a test to see how straight these so-called 'out-of-its' were, he decided to cultivate an interest in the game of Lords. His experiment was an overwhelming success and the result was that Patrick Malone was not only a reject from the society he had rejected, but was also now not accepted by the fringe of society which previously he had accepted.

He and his son had even invented a game which would offend either camps. Called 'Kicket,' it involved using a cricket bat and a ball like a soccer ball, only smaller. The stumps were set in the usual place but instead of bowling a ball in the traditional way the person kicked the ball towards the stumps as though trying to score a goal, a la football. Believe me, one day Kicket will catch on!

'So, here I am sitting on a wooden bench, a rug around my legs, ready to watch another game of cricket. The whole sum of my life is here with me, on this Jeremy coney island wide-screen of the mind. All that has passed in thought, word and deed is now past and here I am, one among many who have also thought, worded and deeded their way through life to this point in time and place. Curious! Absurd! It was just like the theme of the three caskets or stanzas from Wotan ...

All that was I know
All that is I know
All that ever shall be done
This as well I know
Erdna the name I bear
The fates my daughters are
Danger threatens dire
This had drawn me near

Hearken! Hearken! Hearken!

All that is shall end
Heed ye well, ere dawn of doom –
Beware the cursed Ring!

And, of course, Alex PSM could not think of Wagner without also recalling Roy Kinnear and Elanor Bron trying to retrieve the RING, the RING, get the RING from Ringo's fingerario. Oh well, you may use blank canvases or paintings or photographs to do this piece, but I only hope Maureen doesn't leave me and become just another thing of the past. It would probably appear a fairly minor offence to miss a day off work to go to a cricket game or whatever, but I can see how she's thinking. She's afraid of my slipping back into how she thinks I was when I met her, like the frightening bisexual Ur-mother would have him do.

At this point a roar went up from the crowd as the two captains, Jeremy Coney and Te Rauparaha, came into the middle of the area. Eden Park was almost full by this time and the great excitement steadily built as Patrick Alex Malone switched on his radio. Cricket commentary added an almost intangible element to the game and Magic Malone followed every word as though the whole fate and destiny of the world hanged on them, as in the 1911 beginning, for example. It was a bit like the feeling of dying mingled with a voluptuous sensual pleasure.

A DVD is now showing: of a cricket match set in Auckland in the 1970's

'Morning John, welcome once again to New Zealand and welcome listeners. Well, what an extraordinary game this should be. The sun is shining, the Eden Park crowd is sparkling. There are a few dark clouds over the Waitakere Ranges, but let's hope the rain stays away and we can all enjoy this tremendous, spectacular day's cricket. In a moment I'll run through each of the teams but at this very minute I can see Te Rauparaha toss the coin that will decide who will come into bat ...

'Oh dear! There seems to be some sort of controversy brewing out there even before a ball has been bowled. Te Rauparaha looks very angry and he has quite a reputation for what he might do when his feathers are ruffled. I'm a big believer in making the manuhiri feel at home, for example, if the visitors likes red, let them take all the red parts. I seem to recall that one time he was so furious that he went to Akaroa I think it was ... or was it Kaiapoi? Anyway somewhere in the South Island and ...'

'If I may interrupt Dennis, they seem to have taken a bat out into the middle. It looks like ... Oh! How amusing, they are going to decide the toss
by throwing the bat in the air and seeing whether it lands on the flat or the back of the bat.'

'I haven't seen that done since we played at school some thirty or forty years ago. I think it was a favourite practice of the aristrocratic Edward de Vere, Earl of Oxford, if I remember rightly, but I can't even guess what that was about today, can you John?'

'Not for the life of me! Oh well, no doubt we'll find out in due course. Now if I may, I'll just run through the two teams and perhaps we could make a few comments on selection and some of the players' recent form ...'

'Hello, Kia ora, did you hear the one about the fella who ran a fast letter delivery service using a dog. His firm was called Kuria – heh heh.'

'Oh, hello, I'd like to welcome to the commentary box one of our guest commentators, Billy T. Ubufella. And I believe you can enlighten us on the goings on out on the pitch, Billy.'

'Yeah, and gidday Dennis, John, and everyone. I just been talking to John Wright and he is the man who will vice captain the New Zealand team. He said that all the huhah was about Te Rauparaha taking exception to calling a Mäori head a tail and they used one of those ten cents and Jeremy Coney island baby called tails. He won, but Te Rauparaha said that's not a tail, it's a Mäori head. Anyway, he got angry looking like he might eat someone, and so the umpire says we'll do it like when we was boys, eh boys and that's it, like the superimposed figure immediately preceded the Spring, it seemed to work.'

A jpg image arrived at this point

Oliver's Balmy Army, they have come to see the Visage, the Vonderful Visage of Odd Odon. The Swiss cricketer, off-spinner, Bernese 'Elvis' Oberland, love me do in '62, out for a ducky an' all. *Le roi soleil,* say ol' King Sol as though he was still the merry ol' sol from the days of old when they dug up the gold in the days of 49 (destroy the originals, as tho' Holbein the Younger's *dance of death* or the young man and girl in spring had never happened.) 'I'm on th' train, I'm on th' train' Jimi is calling out again, as the wind cries to the tree and the hills and the plane, a pungent *pensée*, Hallyday, was half Belgian and on holiday on this Holy Day of Obligation, took a palmful of paracetamol from what was some exotic evening airline. Not so much grave as positively gravid direct from the cradle, puff puff, huff huff as he made fun of the hrimm, hramm ruff, its not easy carrying all those eggs! As a *pourboire* she was bifurcatingly her truffler of arcana along the Languedoc highway, ready to create a new generation as though the Shoah had never happened, when the order went out to send each fragment to an arbitary address.

In the meantime the Greenwitch was sitting on a cornflake *tristesse*, waiting for Malone to come while it seems that O'Halloran was a Dark Horse who begat Guggenheim and Guggenheim begat Agendath and so on down to the bloom of Viagra on the steel-girded railcar loins, or to put it in cricketing terms, the gulf between Chaucer and Gower can be measured for measure by Gower's hesitation, but, lets face it, they were all substitutes for a deeply frustrated longing, me for him ... Patrick Malone laughed openly at Billy T's story but everyone else around him looked either concerned or confused at what was going on out in the middle.

A DVD is now showing: of a cricket match set in Auckland in the 1970's

Jeremy Coney had also won the second toss and as it was announced over the speaker system that the Out of It eleven had been sent into bat, Malone once again looked at his programme and pondered the prospects of the two teams, remembering the mechanism of creative cricketing is the same as that of hysterical phantasies. Both teams were set side by side in a fashion that you could compare each player by their place in the batting order, thus ...

NEW ZEALANDOUT OF IT

1)Dipak PatelJimi Hendrix

2)Ken RutherfordMonk Lewis

3)John Wright (V.C.)Te Rauparaha (C)

4)Martin CroweOscar Wilde

5) Jeff CroweJim Morrison

6)Jeremy Coney (C)Alfred Jarry

7)Richard HadleeJanice Joplin

8)Ian SmithBob Marley (V.C.)

9)John BracewellHerman Goering

10)Lance CairnsLord Byron

11)Ewen ChatfieldJames Joyce

12)Martin SneddonJames K. Baxter

'Yeh, I reckon he's gotta somehow tap into his mana, e. Seeing he's not allowed to do it in the old way then he'll probably try to look for some metaphorical means, maybe use Sutcliffe's other name, Sonata, as a mantra, who knows? Anyway, he is the man ...'
'I'm sorry Billy, but Richard Hadlee is about to bowl the first ball of the first over of this historical match. Jimi Hendrix takes a look around, just checking who's where through the people haze, because Hendrix knows better than any of us, being from the Burckhardtian tradition, that the painting ends when the surface is covered with nails while the artist might remain still and let the subject's own movement provide the multiple aspects as Hadlee comes in off his short run. I wonder what's going through Jimi's mind as he watches one of the world's foremost strike bowlers moving towards him ...'

Hey man, wow like the white streak of power
that provides the purple haze
which is the universe
propelling projectiles such as the red planet of Mars
towards me the centre
of the star-spangled galaxy
there is a theory such as a reverse energy matter
which interpreted into reality
where you use your blood to paint
means if I flick this switch
that's in my hand in the opposite direction,
Mars will go flyin', I mean flyin',

back through the same galaxy
of time and space and over the boundary of infinity
into eternity, far out man!

'Well Dennis, Richard Hadlee will not be pleased with that. No bowler relishes the thought of being hit for six back over his head, and certainly not off the first ball of the innings.'
'Yes John, you're quite right there. But what a shot! I think even Vivian Richards would take a bow to that. Well, we said it would be an exciting match and here we see right from the very first ball the intentions of this Out of It side.'
'Yeah, their intention is to hit the ball 'out of it' e, heh heh ...'
'Ha, ha, ha, that's right Billy. The question is how will Hadlee counter this? I think Jeremy Coney will be a worried man, even though it really is too early to say what might happen.'
'Well here comes Hadlee in again from the Southern end, I suppose you'd call it, of Eden Park. He really looks an athlete this man as he passes the umpire now ...'

Outside in the distance the wind cries
as the man who is as lost as a child
throws his round red ball towards my bat
which I hold erect, yeah man,
the wind cries because this blood red ball
pierces the skin of the air,
the wind cries merry hell
with the awareness of its own existence,
its totem and taboo, its line and chiaroscuro,
but the ball keeps coming and coming
until it hits my bat mid-on
and I'm running and the wind is crying ...

'After a disruptive burst, brought slowly under control the Mad Monk is home despite a good accurate throw from John Bracewell. So after the single out to mid-on Jimi Hendrix and the team's score moves on to seven only after two balls have been bowled.'

What's an Irishman of the Holy Roman Umpire doin' at a cricket game and what's he talkin' – thinkin' to himself. My darlin' Maureen Malone, I was nothing before I met you and without you I'll return to nothin'. It must be like ashes to ashes except it's man to man in his solitary intellectual transit of Venus. The Malone will return to just being a man without his wise woman's influence and love and tellin' off.' But the radio broke the Malone man's talkin' – thinkin' with an appeal for LBW ...

A DVD is now showing: of a cricket match set in Auckland in the 1970's
'Well that must have been close. Umpire Woodhead has turned down Hadlee's appeal. Hadlee went up, Ian Smith went up, then the whole New Zealand team went up, but Willy Woodhead's finger stayed down as though a stone had been placed under it.'

'Yes Dennis, the New Zealanders will feel deprived there. Monk Lewis can count himself a lucky man to still be standing in front of those three pieces of wood.'

'Youse wanna hear how the word umpire came into being eh, well I'll tell you. It was in India eh during the Raj, when the English were Lording it up all over the world especially in India, eh. Anyway the locals used to think they was funny, the British, as locals all over the world did. They knew how prudish the English were in public (and how prudish they weren't in private I might add, where they more than likely shake hands and converse with hands – as did locals all over the world) ...'

'I'm sorry Billy but Hadlee's just coming into bowl again, to Lewis who tries to flick the ball off his pads, but misses and the ball goes straight through to the keeper.'

'I think that the delivery before last would probably have unsettled the Mad Monk somewhat and that he'll be struggling a bit out there, apropos of little sister ...'

'Yeah, anyway the local word for referee was Bumpyre which meant 'being in the hot seat' but because the English were not able to say bum they ummed and arred, went red in the faces and changed it to arrpire, as it was an Ur-event, after a fashion. However, someone said that arrpire sounded silly and that they should say 'um'..'um'.. damn I've forgotten. (What about umpire said Milligan, an unexploded Irishman who was there and unexplained, almost like a study for four chess players) – anyway – hey! What's the matter John! Dennis!'

The radio commentary suddenly disintegrated into a static sound crackling and distorted but what was really two grown men falling about the small box of a building and trying not to laugh all at once. Watching the last two balls of Hadlee's over the PSM Malone tried to fix his radio, nearly breaking it forever in the process. He was thinking to himself, because no-one else was inside his head, unless you count God and the angels ... Well, that's that. I've lost count of all them angels – but me radio's broke and I can't hear what I can see anymore. That is the first time this ...? What do you mean by that?

That is the first time that this ... ? I don't understand what I'm thinking – in spite of all the rational objections to the inexorable fate he becomes unintelligible, no wonder other people don't understand what I'm saying. Now, let's say it slowly. That is the ... I got it! This is the first time that I have had a day off work, except weekends when I really work and I feel so good I feel guilty. I know that's me Catholic heritage and I'm proud of it! Them Protestants can't have half the fun feeling good about what they enjoy. Even their priests get married and look happy. Ah! Maureen me love, they got no soul ... The radio came on with a vengeance at that moment ...

'Ouch! Me ear! It's that bloody unholy Protestant God again,' groaned Malone.

A DVD is now showing: of a cricket match set in Auckland in the 1970's

'Well we seem to be back on the air again John.'

'Yes Dennis, it seems that it's Ewen Chatfield to bowl from the Railway or Sandringham Road end of Eden Park. We must apologise to our listeners for a temporary break in transmission caused by ... anyway, they were able to make it a very short time ...'

There was a stifled laugh, I mean appeal, and then ...

'I didn't actually see the last two balls of Richard Hadlee, too busy thinking about *La Bête Humaine*.'
More silence and crackling and cackling, then ...
'Neither did I Dennis, but I think we can safely assume that – Oh the scoreboard has moved up to eleven so the Mad Monk must have hit a four. Anyway, I'm sure we can sort it all out, but in the meantime Chatfield comes in to bowl to Hendrix who defends, playing the ball gently back up the pitch where it is fielded by the bowler.'

Malone's thoughts took over his mind again. This time they were more subdued and he realises he had been thinking in Irish for the first time in a long time, no, make it a very short time. He had been sober in thought, word and deed for such a long time that he had all but lost his sense of he absurd as his life had revolved around the absurd reality of a nine to five, commuter, suburban existence.
'I must stop tinkin' I mean thinking like this!', thought the Malone to himself – again no-one else was listening. He turned his attention to the cricket, which was why he was here at all. He hadn't come to Eden Park to hear himself think!

A DVD is now showing: of a cricket match set in Auckland in the 1970's
'... and yet again Chatfield proves his worth to this New Zealand side.'
'Yes, he really does have a marvellous ability to get that line and length very early on and just stay there. We have just seen him bowl a maiden over on his first over of the day. Whilst he lacks the drama and penetration of Richard Hadlee, I think we can say he is a perfect foil for the Great New Zealand medium fast pace bowler. If we can just compare the first two overs as an indication of what I mean when I say sell it to the rag man, I am being analytical yet remarkably affectionate. In Hadlee's first over while producing a confident appeal for LBW, which I guess was very unlucky to be turned down, he also conceded eleven runs. Yet old Charley Chatters ...'
'I'm sorry Dennis, but Hadlee is running in now to bowl to Monk Lewis. In he comes past the umpire and – Oh, my goodness, he's bowled him, middle stump! Well, one can only imagine the black Gothic thoughts going through the Mad Monk's mind at this moment ...'

Ah! How dark
These long-extended wickets and rueful ruins
Where nought but bowlers reign, and night dark night
Dark as was chaos 'ere the infant innings,
The nanny's teaching about sin and evil,
A *Bildungsroman* in reverse as it were,
Was rolled together, as black as the pitch
Itself was rolled. The sickly in-swinger
By glimmering through the low-browed misty defences
Furled round with thy spittle and ropy slime
The ball a supernumerary horror
And serves only to make my night more irksome

As MaD as I am, I am always suspicious of wilful distortion, an external control often provides a regulator, yet, yet, those words which belong to one of the Blair brothers from Otago always enter my head when I am bowled out for a low score and help me calm the immediate daggers of the mind which lead to such thoughts as the dripping carcus of Hadlee impaled on the wickets of my brain which stand atop Gothic Calgary – he lusts after the Bleeding Nun who dances seductively around his writhing body, each movement driving the barbed spike deeper into his body – yet he can do nothing as his desire for the nymph of the nunnery increases – see the smoke of movement as he closes his eyes trying to shut out the beautiful visage, but she moves closer, her perfume filling his head and all his senses maddened by her touch, his agony and ecstasy complete as he becomes the more ensnared in this trap, this spider webb of human passion, she the black-widow of Christ smiling all the while ...

'John, you know I've said this before a hundred times, but what a funny game this game of cricket is! How many times have I tried to fathom my utter fascination for this peculiar sport and really, it's like trying to understand the very mysteries of the universe itself. One could say that form is the precipitate of an older content. Its great struggle between random chaos and calculated order seen played out over a lengthy period of five days, although admittedly this being a one-dayer somewhat condenses the process. It baffles and beguiles me!
'Dennis – Yes, but wasn't that a lovely ball by Hadlee. It certainly baffled and beguiled Monk Lewis – in terms of what you've just been saying he certainly will be returning to the pavilion with a belief in intelligent beings existing outside his universe!
"Beware the man from outer-Hadlee', he will be warning his colleagues, as he heads for the black coffee and chicory mill. I think what you were about to say before that dismissal has validity to a point, although there would of course be little achieved in the likes of Chatfield bowling maiden over after maiden over if there was not Hadlee's penetration to complement it.'
'Of course, I agree with that and you're really just saying what I said in reverse, but I should like to pursue, if I may, the more philosophical aspects I began on while we await the next Out of It batsman. I heard a delightful comment from a BBC commentator, and I think it may have been Christopher Martin-Jenkins, I'm not sure. But, he was talking in an aside to a game between New Zealand and England where he mentioned that Dereck Pringle happens to wear contact lenses on the field and glasses in 'real life!'
'This was a casual, off-hand comment and would have passed by had someone not jokingly made a comment to the effect that 'do you not think cricket is part of real life?' This in turn led to a general discussion about the nature of cricket and real life, and one of them commented that, like Hegel and Schopenhauer, he too saw a tension between the ideal and the real. Now the point I make is where do you hang it after sleeping on it for more than 100 nights?'
'I'm sorry Dennis but the real life game of cricket impinges yet again upon our fantasies as the number three batsman, Te Rauparaha, walks onto the field, waving his bat defiantly over his head as though it were a huata, his head held high as he walks towards the battle.'
'Just while Te Rauparaha prepares himself, I'd like to say a few words about Monk Lewis. He never really looked comfortable and an opening batsman's job is never easy of course. I remember in the New Zealand versus England test series of 1965-66, in the match at Lancaster Park I think it was, the great Boycott

himself went out for four, caught off the bowling of Motz in the first innings. And to top it off scored the score of four in the second innings also when he fell victim to a run out. So, moving back from the memory trace toward the entering perceptions, Lewis is in illustrious, if not enviable company with his four runs.'

A jpg image arrived at this point
at this point it is pertinent to note that the jpg is another Magic Alex invention, a Munchausen Moment frozen in time, making palpaple an ancient pound of phanopoeia, thus the introduction of Dichten = condensare, which means that poetry has entered the equation, and Medici moolah (Mr Money, forever Framed in the wayward or wanward smile of the Mona Lisa in Darkest Gore!) meets the Universal Mind. Eclipse of the Trippety-trip, Epistle to Dip, the strobe-lit fantastic down Satie's *Parade* followed by one pure phrase of Pergolesi, to boot, *wie in den Schnabel gewachsen*, we raise our glasses *encore à cet aster* as Paddles runs in along the path of the moonlight mile into the darker side of the bush-clad landscape, as the Runner paddles in the quaffeuse claims a *Coup de foudre* (Tokio Greengrocer) in such a Gubernatorial cover-up.

The familiar night orb left only a black orange hole in the sky - something is missing and resolved ... the ne plus ultra, the *beau ideal,* the amber liquid that opens the Doors of deception heading towards none other than to the sun, the Daddyless son, and all those right-wing ex-L.S.D. boys in Treasury so afraid of their own past that their illusions are complete. Leave a piece of canvas or finished painting on the floor or in the street and the side of the cone makes, Jim! (c.f. HYPERBOLA) As seen earlier, but now he is Pagininiing his strop to echo the lightning strike of cosmic melancholy, somewhat like the 'interior' Africa of which the new romantics and later Raymond Roussel spoke. *Préservatifs*, save us from the appeasement of existential panic, Our Lady of Perpetual Succubus pray for us, now and at the hour of our dearth as we sink into the *sieste éternelle* ...

'Thank you for that enlightening Kantian *Ding-ansich* information. I'm sure that the Monk will feel all the better if he's listening but our attention turns now towards Te Rauparaha and how many times in recent years have we seen a Captain bat at number three – it just makes me wonder, you know....'

'I'll just interrupt you here John, as Hadlee runs into a slight breeze blowing at his back, he passes the umpire with that magnificent flowing stride of his, and bowls to the Out of It Captain who plays a lovely cover drive and the ball races out to the boundary as Te Rauparaha shows his intention from the start. He's not the kind of player who likes to be held down or dictated to and ...'

The radio commentary was gradually superceded in the Malone's Magic head by thoughts of his own. He had been meditating on the comment about Dereck Pringle and the difference between reality and dreams, real life and illusion. He moomy say he must drink water every day. These were thoughts he had not allowed himself for many moons and he could feel the pull of his former Bohemian life becoming stronger, his sureness slowly subsiding like a seemingly secure stock-bank in times of flood ...

So nothing has changed then, all these years of the illusion of reality, undermined by a single, spring tide of high thinking. The iron curtain had lifted to reveal no security. A short while ago it was I was thinking as one of me Irish ancestors might who had no more book-learning than what you can get at the farm-bog gate, and now I'm seriously discussing with myself, through the catalyst of some comment about Dereck Pringle being in real life off the cricket field because he wears glasses, although when he's on, bowling that round cork encased in red leather, he's in some sort of supposed fantasy.

Then my mind extending the argument to the grand banality of philosophical truth and evil or otherwise and all the time me own wife, Maureen O'Shea, is telling me that I'm living in some sort of unreality, and that I'd better get a job because we've got to pay the rent and eat the food and the baby is only two months away ten years ago and yet here I am ...'

PSM could hear the low-rev chugging of a diesel engine as it struggled up the Kingsland Embankment bringing a train of goods from Northland in its wake. The German word for train is *zug* and means 'the puller'. The emphasis on the power in front rather than the 'train' which follows had always intrigued Malone, as had the Germans themselves fascinated him. He had always thought it something to do with the powerless being enchanted by the powerful, and he had also absorbed their guilt for the grand evil of Nazism and used it as a metaphor for his own, fragmented 'sad young man in a train' vision.

How absurd it was for a headless figure to run, and for a landscape to contain the letters of the alphabet, although he had nothing to feel guilty about except the fact that he was alive and was aware of the fact that you may wear the painted side in or out! As he sat there on the Eden Park Grandstand, watching and listening to this fabulous game they called cricket, and watching the clouds swirling dark and light and quickly across the sombre West of Auckland sky, he knew that his ten year investment in the illusion of the Protestant work ethic was a complete and utter failure, and that condensation underlay his approach to these fields.

I came into this world with nothing but original sin (there's a guy who's got religion, he'll tell you if your sin's original) and it is only God's love and forgiveness which can absolve me, not good thoughts or words or deeds. I am a sinner, always have been and always will be – it is the darkness within which is my true self ...'

Suddenly a roar went up from the crowd and someone pushed Malone violently to his left as a cricket ball came thudding out of the sky and landed where he had been sitting. Malone, who had not seen the ball nearly land on his contemplating skull, was ready for a fight. 'I'm still on the train', he thinks in his Kenkesian ontology, still attempting to render the experience of standing still in a moving vehicle. Like a cobra's head his fist was ready to strike the stranger who had just saved his life. The PSM looked at his supposed adversary and saw a large, smiling Māori man looking down at his crumpled Irish self.

'Soon take the grin off his face!' The misguided Malone said to himself and it was only the intervention of the modern, almost broken transistor radio whose voice permeated the dim, primordial Celtic mind, which stopped what could have become the beginning of a racial conflict throughout the long white cloud – yes folks, it could have been the cloud wars all over again! But thanks to the Irish-Māori view of time, disaster was avoided –a disaster which would have been perpetrated by the Irish-Māori view of a good scrap! As the fist-cobra was about to strike, the sound waves of radio messages reached the Malone's receiving apparatas with the following words of the English language:

A DVD is now showing: of a cricket match set in Auckland in the 1970's
'What a magnificent hit right into the grandstand making that the fifth six off five balls!'
'A stupendous shot indeed from the Out of It captain and ...'

The Malone's mind changed the direction and appearance of his cobra so that the snake-like venom of the clenched fist whilst in full flight, moving swiftly towards its target, became an out-stretched hand of friendship and gratitude. Had Anglo-Saxon clockwork time been used the punch would have landed because the mechanism for change is not an inherent component of the technological age. However, his ability to emulate MaD's explorations which show a particular preference for combining contraries into a unity and reveals the Marey features of slow fragmentation allowed him this notoriety that has never diminished.
The Malone breathed a sigh of relief as he introduced himself to Rewi, who had suspected nothing but what happened.

'..and the excitement is intense as Te Rauparaha attempts to join and indeed make a world team of those who have hit six sixes off one over in first class cricket. The existing duo of Garfield Sobers and Ravi Shastri may soon be part of a trio. Perhaps they'll form a combo and do a world tour, who knows! Of course, they may prepare special food for the piece.'
'Of course Dennis, the remarkable thing is that this is off the bowling of Richard Hadlee, one of the ...'
'Indeed John, and here he comes now, he tries to dig it in short but it doesn't get up and Oh! He's done it! Te Rauparaha has hit the ball right out
of the ground and I'd say that that ball was trying to catch the next train up at Kingsland Station, Dennis! What a shot!'
'Hadlee can't believe it. What a game this is! To have a maiden over bowled by Chatfield followed by this, is extraordinary. Well, this Out of It Eleven are certainly winning over even their most ardent antagonists amongst this Eden Park crowd. Young Ken Rutherford will be saying 'So that's how it's done?' To himself no doubt.'

The Malone went back from listening to thinking. 'That was a close thing – it's all this thinking that's no good – it's unhealthy I think, thus once a year on a snowy evening, place the think-tank in the town square and have everyone throw stones at it, if you know what I mean. What do ya mean ya don't! There I was with thoughts about the Nazi, Irish, Holy Roman Train, about the wife and about sin and guilt all going on and I missed a whole over by Chatfield and five sixths of an over by Hadlee – I even missed my own life being saved and here I am thinking about all my thinking, a factor extraneous to its actual shape.'

'Well, I gotta go bro! I gotta meet my mate Golly!' Said Rewi.

'Thank you again Rewi, I don't know what to say – how do you say anything to someone who saved you from crayons to perfume? Anyway, not wanting to exploit the calligraphic language, did you say Golly?'

'Yeah – he's my bro, we came to the game to see the Chief e! – You know him?'

'I think so maybe, has he got big fuzzy afro hair – Oh, I know he had a sister called Hine.'

'Yeah, that's him e! How you know Goll?'

'I guess we're related – but I knew him years before I married Maureen O'Shea. Maureen is a relative of Hine's husband, Paul.'

'Oh yea I heard of you, e. There was some kind of raruraru between your wife and her family e! Anyway, I'll go now. I'll tell Golly I saw you, maybe we go for a drink or a smoke after the game.'

The PSM was afraid. His mind meandered back through the past and speeded forward to an uncertain future. His stable, safe life was threatened from all sides by the past and the present and the shape of things to come, which were no longer geometric, nor measured by such as quarter-acre backyard birds or 5.15 train. He wanted to run back to a past which had already passed. His thoughts were swimming in a sea of uncertainty where the horizon looks much closer than it seems, like some Spinozarian nightmare. The fish-bowl of reality he had lived in had smashed open and the big fish he had been, now became a small fish thrown into a large, unknown and frightening ocean, where nothing was familiar or certain – if only he'd gone to work he would have made the dream tolerable to the never-sleeping censorship!

Going to the pub, the allusion to smoking dope, the mention of family fights, the magnetic pull of his heroes out there on the pitch – the Malone Alex personality felt like he was being sucked into the vortex of emptiness, away from his Maureen, away from Colleen and Sean and Tahana the twins, and the baby Rua, away from New Lynn and the fenced-in section, away from it all – he was being sucked 'out of it,' out of this world, out of T.V. and Radio, out of the weekly paycheck, out of it he was moving out of his woman's mind and heart, out of his woman's body, he was losing contact, he was heading skywards, having traversed the suburban king and queen with Swiftian nudes he was taking off from the point of contact between Rangi and Papa – the two elements. When he was inside his woman he was secure, he belonged to earth, when he was inside his office or his living room, or his train or his supermarket he belonged to society, when he was – he was!

But he began to feel he wasn't, was not was, his bohemian daze was returning. The time would be in the evening before the lights are lit. Here is Fred saying to PSM he perceives all great works as unfolding dramas of the mind. Thus PSM was the wild wolf on the outskirts of town, he was Rubezahl, the dark ghost of the mist and mountain, he was Magic Alex, he was the renegade, the degenerate, The Munchausen Moment, the uncentred point of the turning world and spinning, spinning, spinning fast and off-centre, he was Schnitzler and Proust, he was Rangi, porangi, haurangi, sky father, sky fool, he was blue and endless, grey and formless, black and eternal – he was heading out, towards nothing, away from everything. He was a bachelor again, striped bare of his bride, even. The Malone was alone – almost man alone, he struggled with the existential void. He tried to focus – 'what about the time!' But he was almost out of it. There was no more time, no more place, no more – 'All this – what? Am I going back or am I staying. Am I at a cricket match or am I going.'

A DVD is now showing: of a cricket match set in Auckland in the 1970's
'What a catch, and that's the end of Hendrix!'
'Yes Dennis, a great take at second slip by the skipper Jeremy Coney and he'll be a happy man. I feel that after a firey start Hendrix just slipped back a little, a few overs without scoring, being pinned down by Chatfield. Then finally getting down to what may be termed the 'action end' where Hadlee is bowling. He hit one four after not really adjusting to the change of pace, and the very next ball caught the edge, the ball went flying at a cracking pace, but Coney's got a good pair of hands and there we are – Hendrix walks slowly to the pavilion, you may use telescopes to watch. I bet he'll be spewing!'
'Well, John, it's a funny old game. I thought Jimi was looking great when he came out to bat. He, as you say, played a couple of delightful scoring shots and, well I can only really re-iterate my absolute admiration for Ewen Chatfield. I know Richard Hadlee took the wicket, I know Richard
Hadlee had the penetration but, and I can't stress this too often, it was Chatfield who tied Hendrix down, got the virgin frustrated, as it were – Hendrix is a player who likes to get on with the game – and Chatfield primed him for Hadlee.'
'We could go on talking about who primed who for the rest of our lives, Dennis. The fact is the two Out of It openers are out. So the score after only seven very eventful overs here at Eden Park is two wickets for sixty-six runs, although I'm sure my colleague would correct me and say sixty-six for two!'
'Ha Ha! That's an old argument perhaps we can revive at lunch John. But at the moment I can see the fourth Out of It batsman coming to the crease. And it looks like we have a change of batting order. Yes, it's Jim Morrison coming out and he's using twelfth man James K Baxter as his runner. Well, what do you make of this turn of events John?'

As the two commentators prattled on the Malone was thinking ...
'I must stop all this thinkin'. To have a rebellious heart at any age is a mortal sin – to have one at my stage in life is just stupid. I'll just sit here for what I came for, to watch the cricket and I'll send the bad thoughts –'
But it was no good. He was 'one who dreams in broad daylight', a Daydream Believer, always monkeying around. Even thinking in terms of bad thoughts was a childish thought, a throwback to his first confession when, after a terrible struggle, he had triumphantly gone to the priest to tell him all his evil and dark ideas which would never have occurred to him had he not been told to go to confession! He was so pleased with himself and could not understand the holy man's reaction of disgust that 'such filth could come from one so young, Holy Mother of God, etc.' He thought he had done what he was supposed to, and he found that when he really tried he could think of anything, no matter how degrading. In this sense it is an image of an event without temporal or spatial significance, something akin to Arthur Dali's *Invisible Man*.
Henceforth the Malone determined to take an immediate interest in the minutest aspects of this cricket game, even if there was a piano for sale. He would follow each ball bowled and that was all his mind would be on. His mind, however, had

other ideas so that the more he tried to keep the dark clouds of chaos and madness away, the more in reality they were there. His struggle of will was enhanced and punctuated by the outside reality. So, the sky darkened over the Waitakere Ranges threatening to move eastwards from the west, thus nature was empathising with the Malone's uncertain internal spirit.

When the sky is filled with them, ask people to shoot. It was like masturbation thought the great Malone mind – 'thinking what you shouldn't be thinkin', but only being able to think it because of what you were doin', which is what you should be doin'. But it's worse if you think about something else and keep doin' that because then you're thinkin' what you're doin' whilst doin' what you shouldn't be doin' or even thinkin' of doin'. Yes, that's it. Catholicism in two nutshells. A grand cock and bull story, it cannot be denied, when told by Mr Quirinus, Tuner. Well, you can but take one of the two yoga positions and see the painting that you like for two days, so say Sufi Joe from his jettisoned aéroplane, Munchen, 1912 surfin' USSR.'

The thoughts were drowned by the crowd cheering, as Morrison hit Chatfield down to deep cover and sent Hemi, grey-hair, grey-beard flying like sails, off for a run through the hole in the door which he had been fixin'. The chief ran like the wind so that Baxter, who was obviously the least fit of the two, was stretched to the limit but made it home for three runs.

A DVD is now showing: of a cricket match set in Auckland in the 1970's
'Ha Ha! I bet that got the old cogs in the wheels turning, John. I thought the old guru of the New Jerusalem was struggling a bit there.'

'Yes Dennis, but he made it and his thinking must be matching his physical triumph at this moment. He is probably thinking 'Saint Leon J. Saul and the three Eilser Sisters, why have you abandonded me,' or some such rosary beaded prayer.'

Man! He has called me again
From that place inside me – the unworthy

Servant! He called me three times
When I, in my mortal dung heap mind

Would have settled for one
And all the lice in my beard jumped out

For fear of this terrible century's (looming) speed
Who will torment me now, at night

Who will remind me of Him –
And sin! Which this mad old devil

Commits with every eyelid bat, every thought
Kei te Rangitira o te ngati porangi, ahau –

I stand at the end of the crease Colin
Knowing He only wants what He knows I can do

'Well, John, it's difficult to imagine Hemi taking a victory easily. His sense of guilt is so finely developed that you can't even imagine him waking up in the morning in the house without Windows98 and without him saying he was sorry to someone. I'd really like to see if he actually thinks in sonnets, like an emblem of the transformed personage, perhaps. I bet even now he is having second thoughts about his first sonnet! He's probably opting for the more traditional form of that particular literary expression, rather than the twentieth century type once favoured by the likes of Durrell. Oh well, I suppose that will remain one of life's imponderables ...'

MAZEPPA 4-4-OST (for VicO'le and the *Scienza Nuova*)
Refrain: *Quando para mucho mi amore de felice, corazon*

Like a child's trick, the upside-down crucifix-bat you'd hung
Above your sofa, inside the door the stage Lucifer unfurls
Crouching, taloned on your back wicket to frighten girls
An apple tree outside solicited Calvin's town well-strung

With big blowsy white flowers. In the big room we discussed
Books, friends, and your divorce; your battered gentleness
Made all the bandages fall off. I saw Mazeppa's recklessness
Roped to wild iron horses with sharp curves, bowls at his thrust

Head, strung up to die on the inescapable cross of the flesh
Anointed with dung, feet pointing to the sky's meadow, fresh
He swung the ball like a bruised doll. I remember you said
You shot the Albatross, Christ, as he hung nailed fast, dead
To my youth's sky. In reply you said it's a Miracle, the bland
Risen corpse of Christ has bled wickets through every land

'Dennis, you know so much has happened here that while I remember, I must acknowledge Te Rauparaha's fifty has come up! In fact it came up a couple of overs ago – and he faced only thirteen balls. I'll look through my Professor Kacha's book of cricketing records but I'd say that must be one of the fastest half-centuries of any batsman in the world.'
'What a cricketer he is! Out of a team score of seventy-eight, two of which have been extras, this man has scored fifty-eight. If there ever was a case of a captain leading by example, this surely must be it.'
'The other aspect is of course, Dennis, that he hasn't taken any unnecessary risks. He's played every ball on its merit and he hasn't been at all reckless. Apparently before he comes out to bat each time he writes all the things he wants to do. Although, as the E.P. from Sus-sex Ludwig Binswanger, observed the image is not a symbol nor the key to dreams, so no matter how stromg your power of visualization might be, you still have to go out there and whack it!'
'Yes, it's the great skill of the man that one has to admire. I shouldn't wonder, John, that his bat will take its place among every other national taonga at Te Marae Taonga o Aotearoa down there in the Capital.'

'It would certainly deserve to be there amongst the rest of our country's treasures and Te Rauparaha is one who is very much aware of his own mana within cricketing circles and the wairua which is part of his toanga.'

'I'll interrupt you there, John, to say that a rather large dark cloud is just crossing over Eden Park and out towards the West things are looking decidedly gloomy. In fact the poetry of the situation becomes impure and if it accepts the dream it can be a numerical figure, a chocolate grinder, an insect or a finger print. The umpires seem to be checking their little devises, known in certain MaD circles as 'Gustave's mother's candle,' as regards the light. It would be an awful shame if this most absorbing game were to be interrupted.'

'Yes John, how true, in the meantime I should like to welcome back Billy T. who has with him Mr Sef Vulu who is a local Auckland cricketer. Gentlemen, welcome. Perhaps Billy, you would like to introduce Mr Vulu to our listeners.'

'Kapai, e, Dennis. Kia Ora Sef.'

'Maloni, Billy and everyone.'

'Count the wrinkles on each other's stomach! As they say where I come from.'

'Well, bro, what do you reckon about this game so far, pretty neat e, hehehe.'

'Well Billy bout this game, it's goot. An' I like to make comment bout this Te Rauparaha so far. I saw him play in Barbados a coupla summers ago an I always like the looka him.'

'Sef, you're like the opening batsman for your own Auckland club, e! Would you like to comment maybe on either Lewis or Hendrix's performance today.'

'Wella Billy I think they both never got off to a goot start. It's not easy opening when you're out of it, an' I think they both try but never get off the ground, a bit like the archaeopteryx being an apt symbol for an old bird like Hanold.'

'You also play Pacific Island cricket. What's the main difference between that and this kinda cricket e bro?'

'I think the numbera people ona field. That, ana I think there's not dancing and singing when you score in a palagi game, and as they say, if there ain't music at the revolution, I ain't comin'.'

'Kapai e hoa. I think it's time to go back to my cousey's Dennis and John, Kia Ora.'

'Thank you, Billy and Sef Vulu. We'll be seeing Billy again later on of course, but right now it's back to the game here at Eden Park where for the time being anyhow the news is good. The light seems to be O.K., although looking westward I think there may be problems later in the day, but I think the umpires want to get on with the game before those 'heathen Christians' arrive on their MaD bicycle wheels holy-rolling, and Holbein's *Lady Madonna* starts trying to make ends meet, yeah.'

'Oh! And there's a terrible mix-up here and Hemi's slipped over with his bare feet and I'm afraid that means Morrison has been run out.'

'Well, there you see the problem of using as runner, John. Morrison called his captain through, probably thinking that it would be on – but judging it as though he were doing the running himself. The chief, obviously eager to push the score along because of the weather, came. But, Baxter without shoes, struck what is obviously a bit of moisture out there, lost his footing and there you are. Like father, like son: bald archer arrowed WW1 out of the Boche Box of 1914 and its dark, dazed mood. I got the CONCH! I got the CONCH!'

'I remember the hapless Geoff Howarth being run out in similar circumstances, Dennis. Howarth had got off to a good start for the first time in ages and then much the same thing happened. I forget which game it was exactly, I always confuse it with the one where Howarth had just moved out of his crease after John Wright, I think it was, had hit what looked to be a powerful scoring shot, but the ball came straight back towards the bowler, just glanced his hand and went into the wickets and the poor New Zealand captain was out!'

'One sees so many games that they do tend to merge into a kind of 'neo-catharis' don't they. Anyway, this is the one which we have our focus on at the moment and as Morrison and Hemi make their way back I can tell you that after twelve overs the score is three wickets for ninety nine runs, leaving the Out if It team one short of a hundred. Morrison in the end scored twenty-three after that lovely performance in the last over of Chatfield's first spell, hitting thirteen runs. Altogether he faced nineteen balls and was at the crease for just over twenty minutes, five of which were not played while the umpires checked the light with their Green Nothing Box.'

'Well, Dennis, Jim will be a little disappointed because he certainly looked in good touch. He played a couple of lovely pull shots which simply raced off to the boundary – Oh well, he'll be thinking of what have been, no doubt, imagine dividing the canvas into twenty different shapes ...'

Cricket is strange when you're a batsman
Muscle get strained when you're alone
Bowlers seam wicked the way that they bounce you
Although they know your muscle's been pulled
Cricket's strange – runners come out in your place
Cricket's strange – then they fall on their face
Cricket's strange – a funny game
Cricket's strange – all right now –

'I'd just like to return for a while to the over before last.'

'Oh yes, that was interesting Dennis, I assume you are referring to the fact that Bracewell's spin completely baffled the Out of It Captain, indeed it almost had him L.B.W. off the last ball.'

'Exactly, John, it was of course a maiden over, and it really seemed to keep the chief – well, almost bemused I think would be a fitting term.'

'Baffled, bemused and beguilded indeed Dennis! One can't help but feel a little *Reinigung der Affekte* has occurred for him. And I thought that Morrison himself was starving in some deep mystery when he walked back to the dressing room. It almost seemed he was singing or talking to himself – one could imagine him doing a self-jig or some similar dance had his leg not been crook.'

'Yes! The words Mystery and Morrison seem to be very closely linked in this game as I look through my manuscript notes. And look at Hemi disappearing down the player's tunnel as though he were entering Dante's Inferno. He's crossing himself in the Roman tradition and whipping his very back with what appears to be a large rosary.'

The Malone listened with empathy and sorrow, and each stroke he saw hit Baxter's back was a memory of his life with the Maureen Hinemoana and their children marked his and hers, memories of a life which he knew he would never live again, save one and press it in a book ... They had not been married two months and she was expecting. Then they had not been married eight months, they realised upon close inspection what the situation was, they then got married. 'You carnt be too carful these daze,' the Malone had thought. 'Shotgun?' Murphy, in his enquiring way, had asked 'Double barrel – we're having twins,' Malone had retorted with his fingers crossed, not realising the prophetic nature of his nature. 'Better luck next time' the Murphy had said after the birth of one single child.

And so it was, that not long after nine months, after the birth of the first Malone child, two twins were born. 'Hopefully, ta the sam farther – never like the case bein' now at this moment contested in the very courtroom I was born at the address of the Emerald Isle whence I cam from' said the Murphy, who had had a life-long interest in the law, you know! For was this not the sam Murphy run foul a the law in the Mercantile Gehenna and him a lawyer. 'You're a liarwyer' the judge had said accusing him a not tellin' the truth, as if that were possible!

Malone's Munchausen Murphy Memories were interrupted by the noise of the roaring applause for the next Out of It batsman. Oscar Wilde strode out onto the field with the confidence and arrogance of a man who has nothing to declare or fear but his own genius as a batsman.

Here comes the great man the Malone thought, a rose colour with a glitter and softness that is cool and motiona entered his sensibilities, thus inviting a certain *Scheinsublimieren*. He had forever thought this of the Wilde Irishman and it forever had him thinking of the greatness of the Gaelsand of one and all of his race, and of one in particular it that's the case. Mango O'Brien he was by name known. He was the reason that Malone and his pregnant wife had been able to buy their very house in New Lynn and he was the reason that should PSM not be able to return to the great domestic life of a lifetime that he knew his family would survive.

For, and let it be said, had not Mango O'Brien and his Polynesian wife and their several children, had they not all lived together in a Zeppelin moored only several feet above the ground on the corner section which was next door to where the newlywedded Malone's house on the one side and the railway line on the other. The fact that no-one would but this house for fear and prejudice enabled the unprejudiced and fearless Malone family to buy a perfectly good, respectable suburban dwelling for a very low and acceptable price indeed.

Mango and Malone and Marisia and Maureen and all the more several children had become a close whänau by the time that the Malone got off the train one evening after the work in time to see the O'Brien Zeppelin casting off from its moorings and sail away into the arms of Rangi. 'Where did the man go?' was the question on New Lynn's lips. Anyway, the small compensation for the Malone family's grief over the loss of their true friends was that the day after the Zeppelin had soared into the heavens and beyond, the house prices in the immediate area had soared also, thus providing in the form of material and financial security what they now obviously lacked in emotional and spiritual nurture since the half whänau had headed skyward, like working studies for perspective reconstruction, Mango calling out as a finality 'Imagine your body spreading rapidly all over the world like thin tissue.'

'See you in Heaven!' Malone called in reply, as if he were FOÇILLON crying out abjectly 'life is form, life is form' and he crossed himself as the wonderment of the inverted pagan palagi imploded into the sky above!

A DVD is now showing: of a cricket match set in Auckland in the 1970's
'... and it's not often you see Lance Cairns give away an extra run from a no-ball John.'
'Quite true Dennis, but the umpire, I think, is a bit worried about the bowlers making a hole just at that particular point at the Railway end of the crease. I notice that Mr Woodhead spoke a couple of times to Ewen Chatfield and that must have been what it was all about.'
'Interesting, John, to see Cairns brought back into the New Zealand team, and I believe it has something to do with the fact that the Out of It Number Nine, Herman Goering, is in such good form.'
'Yes, Dennis, I was talking to Glen Turner just after the New Zealand team had been announced and what you say is quite true. There is, of course, a lot of similarities between these two players on the field. Cairns has his bachelor apparatus, Excalibur, and Goering, while there is a little *Lockerheit* in his style, is a big hitter of the ball also, and both men are useful, second-strike bowlers. The Luftwaffe chief, like Lance, likes to flight the ball, *luft, luft, duft!* and they both excel at the in-swinger and out-swinger which should be facilitated by the cloud cover today.'
'Curiously enough, also John, the two men are not unlike each other to look at, so it should be an interesting contest just between these two, let alone the two teams, although I think the Reich Air Marshall has the edge over Cairns when it comes to black-market art theft and leaving a cemetery full of uniforms and liveries, not to mention the dope scandal. But that, of course, does not concern us as we watch Cairns bowl to Te Rauparaha who goes to come forward and them at the last minute moves back pulling his bat away from the line of the ball which ends up safely and uneventfully in the gloves of keeper Smith.'
'Dennis, I know you're sceptical about my oft quoted and maligned 'mania' for statistics, but if I may, I shall inform our listeners that Te Rauparaha has been at the wicket for a total of eleven and a half overs and has scored fifty nine runs ...'
'Very illuminating, its as if you light a match and watch till it goes out, but Cairns is ...'
'I'll just finish if I may Dennis. In the first six of those he scored fifty-eight and in the last five and a half only one run. He does seem completely unable to play either Cairns, who gets such lovely variation of delivery, and the spin of Bracewell who ...'
A huge roar from the crowd drowns out the announcer's sentence.
'John, how many times have I told you not to talk so loud. The big Māori chief has just answered your 'Statistics' by hitting a cracking shot down to the third man boundary.'
'Makes Harry Lime look like a boy scout! Sorry 'bout that, and he made me look like I'm still in nappies. What a fine shot that was as the Out of It score moves on to 118 for three with two balls remaining in the fourteenth over.'

A terrible example of a human bean I am. It was the Munchausen Malone thinking to itself again. Arlo, Arlo, Arlo, what's going on 'ere then. The memory thought of the melancholy of the once lying on his own bed alone and on the radio is *City of New Orleans*, a famous, sad song about the disappearing railroad blues, and how this train was bound for inglory – and then comes Katrina, the great disappearing civilization scandal. This is what heaven must be like, the Great Mind had thought and the Great Guilt had rebuked and the Great Hand crossed himself with the famous 'mea culpa' – some things are never forgotten even though they were never learnt in the first place.

Such was the place of the Latin in the life of the PSM for it had permeated the distorted Irish cerebral cortex at an earlier age and even though he had never been an Altar Boy, a fact he resented and held as a dark sin in his human heart, he never forgot the ancient archaic language and when he finally left off going to the Holy Roman it coincided with the Mass of English – Sure why did ya leave the Mothar Church Patrick Sean Mika – he replied, 'Who wants to belong to a religion you can understand' – and the petitioner would stare in wonderment at his ablilty to make a 'healthful progression' out of that regressed state.

Now here I sit in cold, wind-swept isolation watching the great game and I'm feeling like it's the end. Since I was the young child I have never done what I wanted. The others have told me what was right and wrong and I just said yes. Ma, Da, Holy Church, Wife, Holy Taxman all say do this and it is done – 'Say but the Word and you'll be free and I'll carry a bag of peas to the pharmacy!' – and here I am doing it at last and it ends in the isolation of the self from the holy human family.

A DVD is now showing: of a cricket match set in Auckland in the 1970's

'Just a small point Dennis, but I have just checked up with Mr Vulu who was here before with Billy, on the greeting he used when he came on air. I thought he was saying something about Maloney who plays for Wellington but I didn't like to take it up at the time. However, Billy T. has nformed me that Sef greeted us in his native Tokelau tongue with the word 'Maloni' which is similar to Kia Ora, or Talofa or just 'hello.'

'Well, John with all this talk about the Māori being the lost tribe of Bryan Boru it doesn't really surprise one that there should be other connections between the Irish and Polynesians in general. If you look at the Irish in London and other British cities, then they're occupying a similar position as the Pacific Islanders who live in Auckland and other New Zealand cities. Of course Ireland was Britain's first colony and remains her last, and not as Bronson 'Marty' Feldman would have it, a 'conflict-free sphere.' So that ... Oh! It looks like Oscar Wilde has been bowled out, but there seems to be some doubt!'

'I think I see what happened, and that is it seemed that the umpire called a no-ball but the bowler didn't hear the call and thought he had bowled Wilde.'

'Well, we do get side-tracked don't we John. But, no harm done. In fact I seem to remember a similar incident in Madras (no relation) in the early fifties in, I think it was the fifth test when the Indian bowler Patel took J.R. Reid's middle stump. But the umpire, who was it?'

'Joshi (I won't failure) it was, Dennis.'

'So it was thank you John! Anyway, it was about the first over Reid had faced that day and he went on to score forty-four in that innings!'

'And, if I may add, he scored sixty-three in the second innings so it didn't seem to affect Reid's confidence – it's a pity Wilde can't hear us but I'm sure he knows –

he's been around the cricket pitch long enough to understand all this, long enough to understand the encroachment of an already labelled world upon our spontaneous sensory and intellectual capacities, indeed long enough to sense a smell of the moon in Prussian blue.'

'Anyway, we're watching Hadlee, who is back for second spell, coming in to bowl to Wilde and ... Good Lord he's bowled him again and this time there's no no-ball!'

'Well, that was a good piece of captaincy bringing Hadlee back. Wilde had really taken to Cairns and Bracewell in the last few overs and Coney had the option of bowling them out and leaving Hadlee to come on in the last bracket. But, I think he's done the right thing because the weather is so uncertain – I mean, Dennis, the fact that fifteen overs have been reached means that there is definitely a game on. In fact, we are now in the nineteenth over and with the Out of It team score being 172 means they are scoring at just under ten runs an over, a formidable run-rate – and this may be one of those games in which the run-rate, and not the final score, could be all important, where the numbered circles indicate the positions of the malic moulds, as it were.'

'I couldn't agree more John. I think whatever happens the New Zealanders have got an uphill battle to make a flute out of them. Well, you can't help but admire Wilde. He was at the crease for just six overs and in that time he scored fifty-nine runs including 5 fours and 4 sixes. I should imagine he would be feeling quite pleased with himself as he makes his way back to the pavilion with that arrogant, manly stride of his, knowing that the artist succeeds by seduction ...

Yet each man pulls the stumps on himself
By each let his be heard
Some do it with a simple French cut
And with unflattering word
Cowardly commentators say 'played on!'
Cutting deeper than a sword
Some play careless strokes when they are young
And some when they are old
Some leave such a gap twixt bat and pad
That the ball, like an arrow of gold
Straight to its target blindly goes
Leaving the batsman out in the cold

Some hit too little, some too long
Some wait for an extra or a bye
Some leave the field almost in tears
And some without a sigh
For each man pulls the stumps on himself
Yet none can answer why.

'I'd like to welcome back to the commentary box Billy T. who's just brought us a lovely plate of mutton bird and cucumber sandwiches and some drink – thank you so much Billy. Now I believe you have something interesting to tell us about the Out of It Captain.'

'Yea, ah, kia ora everyone again. Seems that Te Rauparaha only just made it into the team, despite what his present batting performance would suggest. They got this fella who plays for Central Districts called Titokowaru, e. I was talking to Ian Smith before the game today and he told me 'bout this, e bro. Apparently old Titokowaru has a similar relationship with the Out of It selectors as Glenn Turner had with the New Zealand Selection Panel. Both know that 'life is not easy' and as he whispers a secret to a young tree, they make a cricket bat Out of It and send it to a man who will be momentarily delivered from the painful oppression of the willow. The result is that he rarely gets to play on the international scene. A great loss to Te Kirikiti O Aotearoa, ai bro!'

'Well, Billy, that certainly is interesting. It's a constant source of amazement that this game of cricket throws up new or unknown knowledge no matter how long one has been associated with it through a sieve darkly.'

'Oh, isn't that the truth though Dennis. It really is such a varied and changing world out there on the twenty two yard pitch – these sandwiches are great Billy.'

'Ka pai te kai, e hoa! After a visit to Herne Bay my missus made them, her first experiment with some chance ingredients. I hope you like them, e. Better go, e noho ra.'

'And as we watch Billy go off in one direction I can see the next Out of It batsman making his way out now. Alfred Jarry is something of an unknown in this part of the world, although I believe he's made the odd trip to New Caledonia and Mururoa Atoll to give advice on strong-overarm technique.'

'Makes a change from strong-underarm I suppose.'

'Ha, yes indeed! Further to that, our friend M. Jarry has a few other strings to his bow. Apparently, he invented 'pataphysics'. My notes say the term first appeared in print in Alfred Jarry's play text 'Guignol' in the April 1883 issue of *L'Écho de Paris littéraire illustré*. Jarry, always quizical, later defined pataphysical as 'the science of imaginary solutions, which symbolically attributes the properties of objects, described by their virtuality, to their lineaments.' (*Gestes et opinions du Docteur Faustroll*, II, viii). That great exponent of French cricket, Queneau, has described pataphysics as resting 'on the truth of contradictions and exceptions.' However, Keith Quinn is probably more familiar with it through Mal Evan's big BANG BANG theory; back to you John.'

A jpg image arrived at this point

'*Un être sans raisonnable raison d'être*' indeed, even reason may be without reason, such is the latest *imbroglio* caused by the big *Schrabel* in Hamburg! You know my name, look up my number, or '*Etonne-moi!*' as Bishop Diaghilev said to the actress, Cocteau, bland simulacrum that she was. 'Glass must be full before and after delivery' by GOB, himself, if it isn't Lordy Lordy whose heated argument is like wearing a tweed suit at Cap d'Agde, enough to ignite an *idée reçue*, to be sure, where he would use a name card without a name, and where the *id card* is the source of life energy, the passport to pleasure. They are leaving the land in hungry droves, so it goes if you listen to that voluminous myth-kitty, Billy Pilgrim. However, in moments of pecuniary *inquiétude* Alfred Jarry could really stir up the shit no end. Despite his sexual Stakhanovism his prodigious output required no imagination and was not as onanistic as it sounds, at least that is what I heard from Mme Cornuel, a *bourgeoise* famous for her mordant wit.

'Anyway, Jarry is standing at the wicket waiting for Hadlee. He taps his bat on the ground, sounding something akin to a silver hammer clang clanging BANG, BANGING onto its anvil, which listeners can no doubt hear.'

'It's interesting that, John. The way they place those microphones under the surface of the soil, between the wicket-keeper and the wicket, if I'm not mistaken. It really brings an atmosphere of the immediate situation to those listening at home.'

'Quite! Anyway, in comes Hadlee past the umpire, he bowls and ...'

'SHIT'

'Well, there's no doubt from M. Jarry's response as to what happened. We would like to apologise for such foul language entering the air waves and ...'

'Really, while there is no excuse for that kind of occurrence, I suppose it is the price one pays for the kind of technology we were only just extolling the virtues thereof, like a square piece of net deformed by a draught piston.'

'I couldn't agree more, but we could have been forewarned, as this is not the first time the little Frenchie bohemian has opened play in a such a fashion. Or as another French cricketer, Baudelaire, was purported to have said at the end of an 'innings' – 'give a moving announcement each time you die a little death.''

'Of course, it's easy for us to sit here and criticise. We're not out there facing Richard Hadlee. Anyway for those who may still be confused about what's going on, well, Jarry was clean bowled by Hadlee – out for a city duck, and I do believe Hadlee is sitting on a hat-trick.'

'Indeed, he is! He really is a funky donkey, isn't he! While we watch the spectacle of Jarry storming off the field as he wavers between the sexualist and the foreplay, it may be an opportune moment to reflect upon the career of R.J. Hadlee ...'

'And as Lord Byron stumps his way out to the crease, followed by his follower Hemi Baxter as runner-up again, we can only wonder at this remarkable change in the Out of It batting order. There seems to be a certain amount of uncertainty creeping into the Out of It camp with the loss of those two wickets Dennis?'

'It's hard to say really John. I mean if one looks at the scoreboard then one would think they were in the box-seat, so to speak. I mean, with a score of 172 in only nineteen overs you'd think they could be well pleased with their performance.'

'Exactly, but perhaps they're thinking of the weather, or maybe Janis Joplin is just too out of it even to walk out on to the field at the moment. No-one really knows.'

'Yes, well I suppose that could be the case. Anyway, we turn our attention to the action as we see that Byron has finally hobbled his way out to take up the challenge of facing Hadlee, a task I hear that he won't particularly relish, is that right John?'

'I gather so Dennis. Like a lot of spin bowlers, Byron himself is a very good player of spin with the bat. In fact for his own club – the Club Foot Club, I believe he is actually their specialist batsman when it comes to playing spin.'

'Well, I must say I find it most intriguing and bewildering that he should come out to face Hadlee in full flight – I suppose that an 'out of it' captain tends to know the high 'cathartic' value possessed by just those manifestations possessing the least obvious utility than us mere mortals.'

'Indeed, but let's turn our attention to the game as in comes Hadlee now from the Railway end. He runs past one of the ever increasing seagulls who imagine the clouds dripping, and who quickly fly in the opposite direction, and he bowls to Byron, who!!! Oh! And there's a loud appeal for L.B.W. The umpire has a close look, and yes! He's out! Byron just couldn't move his feet quick enough and the result was that the ball went straight past the bat and into the pad of Lord Byron's bad leg and he was trapped right in front of the wicket, and Hadlee has his three-bag utu!'

'A well deserved, if somewhat fortuitous hat-trick for Richard Hadlee – and that, by the way, takes him into the lead again with his tussle with Ian Botham for a five wicket bag. Botham caught up level with him in the last series with Australia, but now Hadlee has played twenty-eight games in which he'd taken five or more wickets and Botham twenty-seven.'

'Yes, a fine performance and I wouldn't wish to take anything from the great Richard Hadlee, but watching Byron make his way back, one can't but feel that there was a certain inevitability about the whole incident - even a hint of sadism, although it would be wrong to persue that line of thought.'

'Well, it was certainly unusual – one can only guess at the thoughts of George Gordon – sixth Lord of Byron.'

I want another go! An uncommon want
I didn't like my innings so I'd like a new one
But all cricketing rules and gazettes say I can't
'A second innings in a one-day game is not a true one.'
All very well for those with two healthy legs to flaunt
But for those with a foot like mine, it is a ruin –
I think all those bastards who make rules for others,
Whilst in their prime,
Should be sent to the devil somewhat ere their time

'No doubt there'll be some small, vitriolic Byronic stanza making its way through the tunnels and over the synaptic bridges of the great western mind as the poet's train of thought carried it towards its final station – the poem on the written page!'

'How very eloquent, I take back all I said bout you being merely a mouthful of statistics, Dennis!'

By now the great mind of Malone was entering a kind of slip-stream-of-consciousness following Bendon, The Erin go Bra Navigator, or so it thought, into who knows where, and the map must be followed exactly, or the event has to be dropped altogether. In advance of the broken arm put two shovels up against the wall and tell him to take his pick. Two dark faces turned in the flare of the Eden Park lights. Who's dat, the PSMunchausen replied, thinking there may have been a question.

Rewi and Paul Calvert said a voice. We come to see you bro, here have a beer. Rewi, Paul, is that yourselves now and the PSM raised itself in salute – come on mind your steps. The threesome moved down towards the sign 'GENTLEMEN' for that was them, neither MILLIONAIRESS, nor NOBLEWOMEN, nor FEMINIST were they, and PSM followed his friends to the toilet and then whistled his lath away among the pillars. They passed the joint nervously under their slack archway.

-Woa, bro!

-Rewi turned to PSM and asked

-Well, Paddy. What is it, e? What's the trouble? Wait a while! Hold hard! With gaping mouth and head far back he stood still and, after an instant, sneezed loudly.

- Chow, he said, Blast you.

- The smoke from the dope, the poke at the pope, the fania, PSM said politely.

- No, Paul Calvert nee O'Shea gasped, I caught a ... cold night before ... blast your soul ... night before last ... and to hell with you drinking too much draught Rewi, from now on its whiskey or nothing.

-They all nodded as one!

They all moved as one back to the grandstand. Here I am thought the Munchausen Malone at last and at length. Here I am with all the people the Maureen disapproves of and doing all the things she disapproves but I've not liked all the people she's approved of in or out of the family and the same with the things.

-Good game, e bro, Golly be along any minute now. He was the one she least liked ... And here I am.

-Kia Ora, Paddy, ha ha how's it? Long time n n no see, e. Hope you got that missus of yours well hi hi hid. She do do don't like me! – Golly laughed and then brought out a bottle of whiskey and said with a hidden noise – but good naturedly here, draw a map to get lost in the mind!

The Malone's head expanded in consciousness and size as he sipped the milk of his mother land for the first time in as many years and there he was and the rain was fallin' on his face and the tears of heaven rolled down his once again young face, the dew from the South washed through him purifying his inner soul - it is, indeed a great day for the Irish. The four sat drinking and talking about old times and when the sky cleared, their heads cleared and so did the airwaves ...

A DVD is now showing: of a cricket match set in Auckland in the 1970's

'Well, it seems things have cleared up, John, the covers have been removed and here, to a round of applause, is Coney leading his men back on to the field.'

'Yes, welcome back to Eden Park everyone and we return with the news that the game is to be reduced to thirty overs for each team. What does that do to the number of overs each bowler can bowl. Have you worked that out yet Dennis?'

'As a matter of fact I have and according to my calculation things do not auger well for the New Zealanders. Under the new regime, I make it that each bowler can bowl only six overs as a maximum, which means that all but one of the bowlers used so far have been bowled out. So, Hadlee, Cairns, Bracewell have all bowled six overs each and Ewen Chatfield has only one over left.'

'Coney, it would seem, has real problems on his hands. We're coming up to the twenty-fourth over, which leaves seven full overs to play and only one of which to be bowled by a strike bowler.'

'Yes, well there's such a thing in this game as thinking ahead, and although I think bringing Hadlee on to make that much needed break-through in the nineteenth over was inevitable, I feel it was a bit like making a mask larger than your face, or shutting the stable door after the horse has bolted!'

'Quite! Anyway it looks like Coney himself will bowl the first ball back after the break as he comes in on the gentle run-up of his, from the South end of the pitch and bowls to Te Rauparaha who takes a massive swing and the ball goes very high. I think he mistimed that shot and what was meant to be a six looks like it could be ... yes it has been caught by Wright almost on the boundary, bringing an end to a very fine innings by the Out of It Captain.'

'Yes, he certainly made good the saying 'a Captain's knock.' For even though he got somewhat bogged down after his firey start and he almost could not play the spin of Bracewell at all, he put early runs on the board and then, just by staying around for the cathexis of the crease, as it were, he kept the Out of It innings together.'

'I couldn't agree more Dennis and I don't think I'll ever forget those six sixes off Hadlee.'

'Oh, yes, splendid shots. In fact just about every ball he scored off could be a study-piece for all the small boys and girls out there watching. He was at the crease for just over one and a half hours actual playing time and in that time he faced just forty-six balls off which he scored exactly eighty runs. A truly fine innings and whatever else may befall us on this extraordinary day's cricket here at Eden Park, I'm sure that the fine innings by Te Rauparaha, the Out of It Captain will stay in the minds of all those who saw it for many years to come. In fact, there will be some who do not talk about anything else, 'Lucky Lipps' Spencer and his psychic jamming, for one.'

'Thank you Dennis, and as the crowd show their appreciation with a standing ovation, the big Māori chief makes his way back to the dressing room. That walk can often be a very long and lonely one, and as we watch Te Rauparaha one can't help feel the isolation amongst all the adulation. It looks as though he is talking to his bat which is something you don't see from many Pākehā cricketers.'

Kie te anake au
Kei te mokemoke au
Kore rawa hui ata mokemoke
Me kia au puritia koe
Taua kia haere ra muringa te haerenga
E hoki ki te whare kirikiti
Ane taku momoe mongamonga
I raro I te mana ma kaupapa
Kei ahau he poke
I roto I taku manawa a wairua
Kei te anake au
Kei te mokemoke au
Kore rawa hui atu mokemoke
Me kia au puritia koe
E taku toanga, e!

'And as the new Out of It batsman, Bob Marley, their Vice Captain, makes his way out, I'd like to welcome 'Big Bird' Joel Garner from the touring West Indies side, into the broadcasting box.'

'Thank you mon! Shure does seem lika box wid a big fela like me init. Imagine one of them broken.'

'Big Bird, you must be pleased to be seeing Bob Marley out in the middle today, perhaps you could make some comment about his recent performance, as he is not that well known as a cricketer in this part of the world.'

'Oh, shure mon! Yano I am always alikin' Mr Marley's performin'. An' he's the one sayta Paterson one time, ya shud be a comin' in from the carpark Hot Shot, yano, yea! So, then thatsa wot he's doin' an' alla people like it, so then he just say yeah, an' he do it, yano mon! Then ther's tha up an' comin' playerz like Dalbiez Gombrich from Jamaica who, while participatin' ina primary process, moves on to dat point to dada art of cricket!'

'We're just watching Coney bowl the second ball of his so far, successful over. Perhaps he'll be out to emulate Hadlee's hat-trick? Anyway, he won't get it as Janis Joplin plays a defensive shot and the ball rolls harmlessly back to the bowler, who does the fielding.'

'Yes, well, Joplin has been quietly building a score, a bit like her enameled Apolinère days I remember so well in the Chelsea Hotel. She's been there now for four and a half overs having come in after Byron, the last victim of Richard Hadlee's little rout of revenge and in that time she's scored 10 valuable runs.'

A jpg image arrived at this point
The Doogan Super Spirit-Level – Lay it on the human soul
 Watch the bubble in its bowl
 By its rise and fall betray
 Whether you are grave or gay
Thus, the ineluctable whipcrack of DNA
Its strands unfurling like inherent pasta
As though the doggerel of the Malatesta
Thru Universal Glue no longer held sway
No right angles, that's Norian Thoughts
As bees buzz about the Brewster's bower
But lying down is the Fürher of noughts
Anticipating niece Geli's Golden Shower

Sparks flew and the Tales of Festlock and Pastern, the inventors of milk, developed a gourmandising attitude to the dothiepin, the hallucinatory Op Art before my eyes metamorphosised from the mundane yet luminary Bookes of P. Ouidius Naso (the unsophisticated idylls of Picasso) into The Oblomovian divan which was seen as the 'Thinking man's Overnight Sleeping Car' on the Blues Train, according to my halibut father, standing head without shoulders above the rest. As he used to say its not the *coiffeur* but the *woucher boucher* that is the 'real' existential dilemma, that is the cynosure of all eyes as seen by the intellectualist aesthetc of Baumgarten. It's a common sight, but the sight ain't pretty, ride a coffin car all over the city. So, it was not 'My Struggle' that hit the chord but the human realisation that '*To be* is fascistic' and '*Not to be* is romantic.'

From thinkin', ta drinkin', ta stinkin', ta blinkin', the PSM was a kind of emotional merrygoround the Mulberrybush, it's along way ta Tipperary an' all! Little did he know he was havin' a Munchausen Moment like MaD, standin' on a mountain, pissin' in a fountain, wit' his best R Mutt by his side, eatin' doggeroll. And for a gentleman Irishmightyodd – he was! But now he had the Rewi and the whiskey, and the Paul and there was talk a playin' pool, and then there was Golly and the lollie, and talk a the girls: he was far away and he knew it.

This was the way they lived and their women bore the burden, but this was on the way in good company and he could not hold back the feeling of tears and laughter. He had had the guilt all the life for doing nothing, now at least he could feel the guilt for something he had done. From the moment he had decided not to go to the work, that was the time he had fired his first blows against the empire of tyranny he has suffered under.

If it meant being an outcast, a wife and child deserter, if it meant loss of all privilage and place in society, if it meant emotional isolation, the loss of his woman's love, and spiritual damnation then so be it, that's what it meant – another dram me boys, he watch the sun until it becomes square and the PSM with his traveller's folding pack, and his fooney ballooney hat rack, he open his trap and drank as if it were the beautiful stream of conscious life givin' water that it was, just like IN HOLLAND, the 5th of November 1968, where Alex followed Fred to a large field of MM's but did not go beyond! Now here we are on that same day forty years later, remember, remember, the 5th of November, BOOM! At least she didn't go off with whimpering, soft Eliot thought Bruno as he emerged from the kitchen cave to bring Alex his lunch-munch and his lunchtime Munchausen Medication, BOOM! BOOM! BOOM!

A DVD is now showing: of a cricket match set in Auckland in the 1970's
'Yas mon! Shure isn't it a pity that Bob Marley lost his wicket, I thort he was lookin' pretty good there. He hit himself a six, then four and then well mon, if I hud ma way I'd just say shure is a pity. I'm sayin' it may be da herb or it may be da rum anyway I'm sayin, dis for a fact, Botham shuda been in da outa it aleven, but he's justa finish playin' for dada ashes ina Australia.'

'Yes. It's interesting that you say that because I would have thought him a natural selection in the evolution of this team! What do you say John?'

'Indeed, Dennis, but then if I may just cut in here, I suppose we could find so many candidates for the Out of It team. We've already discussed Titokowaru and I personally would like to have seen Sam Becket selected, but there you are, we'll be waiting for God knows until that happens. After all there can only be eleven chosen, and when you think how many Out of It people there are in this world, well it makes me glad I'm not one of the selectors.'

'Oh, yes John I agree entirely. It's interesting to note that all the members of this Out of It team are dead. Perhaps they've taken a more hard-line definition of the term Out of It. Personally, I feel it's a far too harsh an imposition. Good heavens, there must be all sorts of characters in this world who are completely out of it, in their own way, and could never be considered for selection. Why, even you and I John by the end of a day of gin and tonic in the commentary box could be eligible at least for the second eleven!'

'Ha, Ha, by Jove you'd be right there Dennis! Anyway my turn to give a few statistics and to tell you that in the twenty-fifth over we saw the Out of It 200 come up on the board and as we watch Marley take a walk through the gate in the picket fence, I can tell you that the Vice Captain made ten runs bringing the Out of It score to 210 for eight after twenty-four overs.'

'Perfect on all points except you forgot to mention that he was clean bowled, middle-stump by Martin Crowe.'

'Oh! You are an awful pedant, not to mention presumptuous, as with the largeness or smallness in the contents add up to a kind of *ideational mimetics* – and I was just coming to that, Ha! Ha!'

I wanna big score
An it's alright
I wanna hit four
Every day an' every night
Shots to the boundary
And a six right over your head
Is it four, is it four, is it four
That I'm scoring, is it four, is it four, is it four
That I'm scoring.
I wanna know, wanna know wanna know now!

'Well, after the whimsical reggae rastaman the vibrations change somewhat as the Reichmarshal, arguably the most Out of It all his team with his sculpture for travelling luft and all, takes to the crease. The first ball he faces from Crowe sees him on the defensive. Oh, while I remember, Big Bird said to give his farewell to the listeners, he said he wanted to catch up with Bob to get some sort of telephone or some such 'number' to loosen the concomitant of his mental processes.

'Anyway, the point is it was a pleasure to have him up here and I can just glimpse him going through the carpark as Crowe bowls the last ball of the twenty-fifth over which again has Goering on the defensive and the score is now the same as it was before, 210 for eight wickets.'

-Hold on ehoa, says Rewi. Stop.
Before he drew his hand and made a swipe and let fly. Mercy of God the sun had just burst through the Auckland sky and was in the PSM eyes or he'd have been left for dead. God, he was near sent into the country graveyard nigh, how and when it became dirty and why? Sure the Malone took fright as Rewi told him he nearly took a swipe at a Mongrel Mob about the ear like hell, and all populace shouting and laughing as the foreseen event was stopped from having him (the Malone) dragged along like an old tin box clattering along the street ...

A DVD is now showing: **of a cricket match set in Auckland in the 1970's**
'Well, that's the end of Herr Goering I'm afraid. He never got off the ground, like an old sea lion he just sat ticklin' his Tu'm, he never quite got beyond the pleasure principle, basking in the sun, which incidentally is now shining brightly here at Eden Park.'

'Yes, well he was there for just over three overs and he never played a scoring shot, so it is possible that he's just a bit too Out of It, although in the match last week against N.S.W. I think he made a half century – anyway he's looking furious with himself as he storms off the Park.'

'When I hear the word cricket I reach for my revolver!'

'The New Zealanders will be pleased with the lower run-rate, as the tail-end has barely wagged, and with only two overs to go and the weather improving all the time, they might be feeling that they've got a game on their hands.'

-Hey man! You some kinda out of it fuckwit or what. You know I was with the Blacks – why you take a hit at the MMM for – eh! He push the PSM almost over.
-You just a trash, man! The Malone is loose and confused and left alone he is on his way. He looks for Golly and Paul and Rewi but he can't see beyond his eyes. He is walking up now past the Shamrock rest home and his eyes are full of tears and aloneness and he doesn't know who he is or where. He is on a train which takes him further away from New Lynn. But he is already there – away! And he turned on the radio and it said that the Out of It score had been 222 or Nothing and that James Joyce, like a true Tom Swifty, had taken two overs to score the Nothing and Janis Joplin had scored twenty-four – there had been ten extras – so make a number list and hang it on the wall, then read all about it!
The Malone walked across the Once Was Beach and into the Station Hotel, everywhere were telephones which had his number in New Lynn written on the inside of the receiver but he knew that to have a drink would be the easier, more courageous thing to do, and so he sat or stood the best he could all day and into the evening. He, the Patrick Sean Mika Munchausen Malone, danced, sang, played pool, kissed women – all with the tear in his eye. Then the darkness descended and the shadows cast by ready-made clouds making the cold come on to the world like a blanket, invisible and perceptible at once. Malone looked at the money he had left and walked back across the Beach to the Railway Station, in front of which stood the vigorous curves and spring of the pillar which afforded him joy by reminding him of the qualities in himself and the pleasure he derived from seeing them in an other. He went to the ticket office where he bought a single ticket to the Wellington and as he walked towards the train which waited for him until 7.30 pm he could see next to the small Post Office two telephones into which all he had to put was two ten cents (which he had) and he would be connected – he glanced back at the telephone, to be looked at with one eye, close to, for almost an hour, then he headed for Platform One and with the tear still in the eye he boarded the south-bound train which pulled out from the station not long after and he, the Malone of the North by Northwest, inheritor of the tradition of the ashes – in up to his ankles – defender of the faith, went to the dining car and drank whisky, for they didn't sell whiskey, into the night during which nature finally called in her remorseless way and he went to the end of the dining car where the toilet was situated, the carriage was dark, for it was by now the middle of the night, he, the bladder-full Malone opened the door and walked through ...

A jpg image arrived at this point
My moral *rétroviseur* I, Min Kyoung Lee, am a dancer, choreographer and performance artist based in Auckland. I have been presenting my own dance and performance works in 'Lateight Choreographers' in 2004 and 2005, and 'InvAsian', an interdisciplinary performance/installation event in 2005. The

choreographers I have worked with include Shona McCullagh, Douglas Wright, and Lisa Densem. I received DanceWEB Europe Scholarship 2006, Unitec Performing and Screen Arts Scholarship 2001-2003, and a six months residency in Akademie Schloss Solitude in Germany later this year. Drachmae Ed and I have worked together in various productions previously, including dance video 'Woven' (New Zealand International Film Festival, Greece Thessaloniki Dance Film Festival, Body Festival Selection) and 'Capturing Twilight', an audio/video/physical improvisation performance as part of Body Festival in 2004. Make all the clocks in the world fast by two seconds without letting anyone know about it and Echo down the decades Mister Ed as a cameraperson and collaborator, and myself as a performer, director, and collaborator, we are intending to create a video art. This work, currently entitled 'Three wives, meditation and motion sickness' (working title)' will be exploring the different perceptions of reality and value, experienced by holding a hand stereoscopy ...

Bottleo Claret fortyouiflhadrealized ... Well, doitnexttime. I forgot about it, George, I'msorry. Willyouforgiveme? Yes. Camptown ladies sing dis song, doodah, camptown racetrack five miles long, doodah, doodao day, you look happy, eyeless in Basra! Happy? Happy? Ah, yes, I remember, now my little Komandant! Gwane run all night, gwane run all day. Put my money on de Brogdingnag, Sambo bid on e-bay! Alex Te Ariki Rubezahl found himself in Ward Number 9 ... then there's this Welsh Rarebit wearing some brown underpants ... about the shortage of grain in Hertfordshire. Now they know how many holes there are in the Sugarplum's bum, everybody's got one. Everyone of them knew that as time went by they'd get a little bit older and a little bit slower, but ... It's all the same thing, in this case manufactured by someonewho's always seen it umpteen times ... Your father's giving it diddly-i-dee/districtwasleaving while he was leaving me ... Intended to die ... the Ottoman umpire says OUT! ... long gone through ... I've got to say, irritably and ... floors, hard enough to sleep on ... per day's MaD in our district. There was not really enough light to get down and ultimately ... slumpeddown. Suddenly ... They may stop the funding ... Place your bets. The original. Afraid she'lldie ... Great colours for the season in the dayroom of Ward Number 9. Who's tok now? Who was to know? I sustained nothing worse than? Here come Fred and Bruno, they want to make him well, you know I love you honeychild, there's nothing in the world I wouldn't do for you, sang-fred in deep baritone meal, whose orientation was humanistic. Also, for example, whatever you're doing he went on to warn that one should not permit oneself to be led astray for medical purposes, although that was sung by Bruno, and to a completely different tune, naturally. A business deal falls through, I informed him on the third night said Alex, when fortune gives us, as Fred so glamorously expostulates, the professions of secular ministers of souls, they don't have to be physicians and must not be priests! ... Peopleride, peopleride. Ride, ride, ride, ride, Lydia Lipovska and Sister Mary Leo ride on the Number 9 BUS to the NY Met, yet ... I've missed all of that too said Fred, I was always thinking about the future of an illusion (1927). It makes me a few days late, compared with like, wow! And weird stuff like that, but Bruno reminded Alex of the poet H.D. who, while talking to the animals, referred to Fred as the midwife of the soul ... Alex thought he must be taking our sides sometimes ... Rubezahl also remembered the floral bark Moulin Rouge (1943), and how the doctors had brought this specimen that had nobody's short-cuts, aha, to the The Internal Soldier: (a different kind of soldier's tale), and here is the struggle of Paul Joseph. Fred insisted he is a different kind of 'Unknown Soldier' to whom there is no mon-u-ment, except, perhaps, the writing of Arthur Schnitzler ... Frag-men-ted ... No-one can understand his ... nightmarish existence ... nor his attempts to be free ... He mihi aroha, kia koe, taku hoa: no reira, Haere, haere, haere Krishna, got nothin' on you, just keep you crazy with nothing to do. Bruno insisted that for these and many parallel reasons that he was talking metaphorically as a way to deal ... with the situation ... They are standing still. The plan, the telegram sent by a man without terrors from beard to the false address, as the headmaster reported   to   my   son. He really can try, as they do, to find function and or form. Here Fred put in his tuppence worth. When I say 'I' I mean my entire self, but for those on an ego trip they are likewise on the, say, Luftwaffe flight to the eve of destruction, as with the adjective *egoistisch*. Here Bruno allowed himself a wry smile, giving Alex a nod and a wink ... You could tell what he was saying, and his voice was low and his hive high. And his eyes were low ... Alright! It was on fire and his glasses were the same. This thing knows if it was tinted. But you know it isn't, Tomeitis, the disease of bookwriting ... So, last night the wife said, oh boy when you're dead, you don't take nothin' with you, so we'd better go to see a surgeon to price it ... Yello wunderclothes. So, any road, we went to see the dentist instead, what a north and south, blimey wot a mouth he's got. Who gave her a pair of teeth? Right said Fred, look at it this way, it is a cultural achievement somewhat like the draining of the Zuyder Zee, which wasn't any good at all to Alex for he would have used the more appropriate *Urbarmacbung*. So I said I'd marry, joined the fucking navy and went to sea. In my broken chair, my wings are broken and so is my hair. The Munchausen Moment is twirling and I'm not in the mood for whirling. How? Dogs for dogging, hands for clapping. Birds for birding and fish for fishing. Them for themming and whim for whamming ... we were chasing that cur, now only to find the night-watchman unaware of his presence in the building industry which allows financial lymphatic limbalance askew in a kind of *Kulturarbeit*. Alex Rubezahl Te Ariki remembers thrusting the blade between his shoulder blades, and that is the reason he is here in the Cellphone Tower Number Nine. As he said at the time of his vigil, if I cannot move heaven, I will stir up the underworld. Both Fred and Bruno could see their charge entering into another world, he was drifting towards the evocative dance, *Die Traumdeutung*, The Watusi, The Twist, jitterbugging towards Eldorado. Take this, brother, may it serve you well. Maybe it's nothing! What? What? Oh ... Maybe, even then, impervious in London, maybe because I'm a Londoner ... could be a difficult thing ... It's quick like the rush for peace is, because it's so much like being naked, eating roast beef, whilst watching the Queen of England's Christmas message on TV, her majesty's a pretty nice girl: It'salright,it'salrightIt'salright, Beefeater's cocaine it's alright, it's the vision which, black as pitch, only Alex can see now, as the others look on, and Bruno is whispering to Fred, *Feblleistung*. Ja! said Fred. For dinner tonight its beef Stroganov made by our cook, Mike (round the world in a Number Nine Bus) Verne, whose motto is ...

That those eat now, who never ate before

If, you became naked …

brrm brrm, rrring rrring rrring the peace fulpoe tic scene of wordandsnow was suddenlyshattered by ifit isnt pitaedith backa gain riding shotgunwedding on the back ofa Harley and at the apehangers steering and heering and swearing is her boy friendfrom the notorious patch honki toothfairy (himselfthink always think edith wasa way with the fairies) … they roarup and stop, honki takes a swipeandaswig, he has tattooed on his forehead 'tobe or not tobe is hard for the people,' thus indicat ing he is a member of the literary mob, but as long as people do not know about it, nothing is disturbed … he hands the bottle of whiskey toedith and himself catches the faintly the words 'i roto i te koraha pore kau he potae' (himself the remembers the blightplight ofhis ownones who cameto him with the story of beingin the wilderness without a potatoe and he laughsandcries) honkicomes over to himself and pours a large draught of the water oflife down his throat it is all he cando, 'Gottago bro, you just like us, e, laughing and crying at the same time, kia ora begorrah e hoa haere ra!' hehops on the bike andtheyreoff, and as the soulsoothing whiskey permeates thebody of himself every cell in his body is resurrected from death and soned at the sametime the living is easy, fishyjumping brrm brrring brrring brrring honkiedith off towards where the sunset would be if it wasnt aftermid night 'we gonnalet it allhang out' are the last things he hears with ears … con fusion … arthurormathur … the poemere turn, but now dis join ted … his head swims from brainawashwithwhiskey … as unchained manacles release chained limbs … the manu o aroha was about to express its new freedom … the penis mightier than the words butboth areof course connected to love and words lastlonger … army Amagh 1 hope the little ladycomes by whatever method (I got rhythm) 'there's noloving onlyfucking' orat least Sam thinks before hekicked that becket agin but shehas otherideas I daresay from heresay or should I sayas I heard hersay before I kissed her goodnight as passionately as cir cum stances allowed, *elle a chaud a cul*, you can tell by the way she smiles … and now I dream andwait and its the greatmind of himself, *hunani nihil à se alienum putat* te wahi moemoea of herself and he can see his mind is begin ningtogo as hesees her and her sister and her sister's sister and hersister's sister's sister and soon until there are twentyorso in arow like an arrow atahua tatou and heknows his mind follows from nowon the ancient celticsym bols (inspect her) from the book of Kelly's whose whirlpools and whirlwinds weave and wind from within and without in continuous travelfingand unravelling of knowledge and understanding now lost nowgained, the kellywho brought it from Dub was Lynn (new and grey for that matter) the darklin of the formerlin and then the lin of the latter getting darkerstill as time goesby you must remember this, and the old mind infuses the air like a karanga influences the ear which hears … aline is drawn alongwhich travels the thoughts and feelings falling and failings of a generation butit is not the straightline of historical accuracy … itis the mystery enveloping (no prizes for guessing what), set each one to an arbitary time, arbitarily, or according to a system that you make … but, himself, looks up tosee the oldwoman whocomes walking pushinga bike uphill and shesees himself lying there and is happy to have someoneto talkto … shelays her girisbike down and starts 'Are youa

Cataholic now?' he noreplies (happened oncebefore) and soshee (bar but not banshee yet noone screeching night mareily across the barren wastelandyet) asksa gain 'Are youa Cataholic, then?' Thennow the savage nowthen reply of himself (in his mind, off course), with the recent exception of *David Ricardo*. 'Well, 1 like cats, especially blackpussey, yes but I'm no fan attic,' and she, who hassettled in says 'well I'm not talkinga bout supersititition but religion' and he 'samedifference' answersing face eatiously (what mouth whatamouth) she lookshurt but explains to hisquest ioning that she has alpineclimbers disease and is forced to wanderin the heights for the restof her days and nights, no rest for the whickers or any other baskets from the Blaskets or whereabout, so shesays would youlike a ga me of Spoil Five and pullsout the pack of cards ... I cannot play sayshe (himself) ... just listen, she explains, highest ina redsuit, lowestin a blacksuit, takes the trick ... two of spades beats anyten, except diamonds ... knave of the ownsuit, trump beats kingand queen ... but the five of the suitbeats alleven the jack ... aceof hearts has specialpowers canbe beaten but trumpace, knavefive can cross suits! playedfora pool eachrounds ... object to stop others winning! ... I cannot play, himself re it er ates, somehow point ingto his mangled hands 'Oh,' she says 'Well I'd bettergo, I'll tellyou this' andhe listens to Moi, no Rita by the metre made, tell herstory to his ... its like she's not there at all, it's like sheishim, like hermad ness has mingledwith his, so what sheisaying is coming from inside his head ... being the last of myfaminerly and not livingin mynative land I williamtell of things that apple between myeyes other wisewould belost forall times, therefore I live accordingly, remembering the full of romance and *Air de Paris* like a preliminary study for Tzanck, who eloped with Rrose Sélavy (only a rose, Ivan the Red, its oonnllyy aa rroossee) out the fresh French window on a night like this ... succeeding generations mayask whoam I, manor woman, wheredid I comefrom, woman orman? ... by this I hope I will beable to help those see their pre deces sors against the back dropof lifeasit wasin Ireland in those days, for the necessity of ramsacking my memory and invention, for all sorts and combinations of periphrastic expressions, as equivalents for modern ideas, images and relations of things the people whogave them faith, loveof Ireland andits culture through the upsand downs of the troubledpast, we've had toem igrate becauseof the existing con ditionsin Ireland which brought bus iness and trains toa standstill ... what was knownas the Suezcrisis finallyde feated us aswe owneda garagein Chapelzod, the pig bigoil comp anies swallowed and swilled the small bus inesses by curt ailing petrol under theguise of short ages, whenin fact the oiltankers were fullout side Dublin Bay... wewentto Ballyshannon to say fare well to our loved ones (there was a waugh on!) a heart breaking experience and when we got to Newzealand ... at this point Rita pointing to points' north said she must begoing forshe had morealpines to climb and as she headed northandsouth, eastandwest pushingher little bike dearold tyke had she beena child it wouldhave been a trike whichit was because shewas ...

Here Joe Blogs writes his own personal views in Joe's Blog:
He knows where it is (grrrrrrrr), it's the clan from the girl who commmitted suicide last year. And, because there are 2 80 year old people - it just took time for them to think whether they want anybody to see our Archididascalus. I DID NOT want to press the matter! So, I went there every day, after that tuesday, when I wanted

to leave - so they could get to know me - because they all just weren't there at one time. Two days after that Tuesday, I came back, Munchausen was away and I locked both front doors. I never would have thought she doesn't have a key to HER first door! With me, each house is safe - I lock, even double lock! - as a woman by herself on the road, near the Hotel Occidental - you DO such things! Guess what happened: she came home - I was on the toilette and didn't hear her, and she was running like crazy screaming she couldn't get into her own house, if no *definite* boundary can be assigned to one's power, the spirit of hope and pleasure makes it virtually infinite ... now, the continuing story of Richmal Munchausen's scathing satire of the FAB FOUR. Last time we saw how Johny and the Moondogs became a howling success with a drummer named Pete! This woman really likes (or should that be licks!) solid young bodies –

'The Argonauts piled into the car, waved to the Outlaws and drove off. Dazedly the Outlaws watched them out of sight. Then suddenly they seemed to be galvanized into action. Their solid young bodies writhed and squirmed in ineffectual imitation of the Argonauts. Their voices rose, nasal and strident, against the beating of the drum.
We've got a 'lectric razor, boys
We've got a 'lectric razor
Yeah! Yeah! Yeah! yelled Douglas
Shouting, yelling, beating the drum, stopping only to retrieve such of their equipment as dropped from them in their flight, they made their way in running leaps along the road.
 We've got a 'lectric razor, boys
We've got a 'lectric razor
Yeah! Yeah! Yeah!'
That's it for now, yours, Joe.

I have more stories shecalled backtohim (shecalledbacktohymn) and himself could hear the turaluratingalingling of herbell (or) and he wasa lone but not for long (not Fellong your working for is it Joseph, notforlong) nolonger than a furlong away as the duck flies or the riverruns past no itsnot green, see, its or time flows or rooffloors, or opendoors, anywaywhat should happen but didn't the sky openand the cloudsparted and a loathsome noise some miles away heard from a child of the bishop, who carried himself in a sort of *noli me tangere* manner, unlike the Earland the Banshee, whose crys more resembled wailing songs, as sung by the beautiful voice of Temoins O'Cult himself, and see, shanties and ballads and the like, singing deathsheads sheepskulls spinning and the terrifying gigglingwhirl all the while as the lightning flashes but is unheardof because of the miles away which it is out over the seeto the east (and Hinemoanat is the son?) ... te marama reveals herself from behind her cloudyvale, showlight enough for life, not for love ... the earland the Banshee went to town wrappedup ina brown paper train, and never came home again ... whirlygigs and gigglywhirls serves you right you gigglygirls, ticaloon on a lunatic world one, two, three nowtwirl ... throw a stone into the sky high enough so it will not come back and suddenly the sky burst open through a hole in a largelightning flash and fourlargefingers and onelargethumb, the hand of God noless, came down and plucked himself from the cold desolate earth and transported him Deus ex machina ... Deus ex machina shelanded, the little nun (answer to the ancientquestion, whatfun do monkshave) Sister Mary Himself, topshelf, heresto your health, she sneakedinto latermasslate and onlyby stealth wasun detected, delectable though shemay havebeen had shenot sworn to have worn habbits which meant she hadbits which you wouldn't haveguessed unless you offered (or if you prefer proffered or more properly poppered) certain uncertain conjectives andor refutations ... anyway being late for masswas definitely out of habbit (what had shebeen doing out of habbit I askew) and S.M.Himself knew that you could onlyblame the hand ofgod so far, there wasno excuse, excuse me she said as she pushedpast (but gently sister, gently, pax ta, and thankyou too went the Samoanpoet) ... so she got to herseat she knelt downon the kneelers called herknees, omcnees being her maiden name, and she begat to pray mea culp mea culpa mea maximaculpa are you alright, alriiiggghhhtttt, sister she heard a voice whisper which thought she had the hiccups and the Samoan looked shockedand off ended at hearingsome one men tion big things in church especially a woman of the cloth, maypy shehas other happits like rappits Paxta thought trying piously to laugh not, how bizarre ... but Sister Mary H, as one of those Irish swindlers running away from their debts to the Isle of Mandolin, was preparing (prepa ringing somewhere in her bi psyche the litle green wheels were following, ono not I again stabbing that picture with a David Bowie knife where, will it end? It could easily decapitate art lovers who came too close. MaD Samsung he went to Perth waiting for his own birth through county Clare mea Clare mea Clare mea maxima Clare, its a boy tits of milk to feed him, Samuel is born and is borne around but the father petersout cant stay the distance of this dance of another wahine toa, taku tuahine, kia kaha, kia aroha haere kia taku manawa, hokia mai kia taku oranga - ka pai, tino pai tau tamaiti, taku iramutu - Samuel Becket is born!) for her confession smoke everything you can as you are sustained by blackberries, hips, haws, and the casual hospitality of strangers ... should she goto communion with such blackstain on hersoul, normallynot, but this was different! (there's avast deferens between menand women ma frenzy, but this time nun!) forit was the thirteenth dayafter death and she was nothingif she wasnot super stitious, thatis she believed! She dida notherquick act ... and then one of contrition once again she knelt at the altar asa bride of Christ withher mouthopen, readyto receive Hisbody ... Preasta, quaesumus omnipoteus. Deus (she was trans ported): ut anima famuli tui N. (famulae tuae Nnnnnn) ... as the priest droned onshe started feeling agitated, her ordeal, a raw deal to be morep recise, was not longa way ... how was shego ing to con fess cosi fan tutti that she had been dead for 13 days and that she wasa man to boot ... the absolution took place on P1820 because the body wasntin church, but she, much to everyone's disgust (isafucken discustard, halloweenaloaya iseseen de MOONBOW!) shelet outa large giggleand a nervous fart, to some extent stifled by the gigglethough those closeto her knew it - she blew it, luckily she was wearing *belle haleine, eau de voilette* for as we have gleaned as species over many milenia of trialand era, absinthe makes the fart grow Honda ... she knew the body was in church on the thirteenth, somewhat changed itis true, but there nun the less ... collect (put in apocket) and cut a hole in the centre of your Weltinnenraum, and why not sneeze while your at it ... Sand to rum at que electro rum, sodomy and the la ah ash ... et rorum (largegirl, lookalike largiri) miser cordiae tuae peremnem infudas. Per Dominum ... canyou keepa road secret that's myjob said Father for I was treated with a respect not

Jsually paid to purses as light as mine ... secreta munera ... Quaesumus Domine quae tibi (quae tibi? What kind of talk is that! Who let the rat in?) pro anima famuli, my family and other animals to you, tui N. (famulae tuae N. here's nottwo tuis in the trees), offerimus placatus (nothing can placate us!) intende: ut remedis pur-gata caelestibus (publica de transporta of heaven!) in tua pietate re-quiescat. Per Dominum (as usual) ... soit came to postconununion tui rua o nga rakau ... and where bound yes we are ... Susipe Domine preces nostras pro anima famuli tui N. (formulae tuae N.): ut, si quae ei maculae de terrenis contagus, as she followed the words as they followed each other through the black mass book, missal if look at it, missile if you throw it, she felt the great surge of passion re kindle that she had for her wife (not her wife) when she had been a man ... Seotho, a thoil, na goil go foill ... he would sing to her, soas the priest was talking of contagiums she was think ingof hush darling ... adheaserunt, remiss ionis tuae misericordia delantur. Per Dominum ... Seotho a thoil! na goil go foill, Seotho, a linbh, a chumainn's a stor ... S.M.H. was nearly crying somuch was the passion for his love but herehe was with a woman's body and living around the time of his future wife's (not his wife) birth, she looked out from the place of worship and saw a brandnew trolleybus (trolleybyceeee mygoan cornrade, and the noise of the rats made a prodigious echoing on the spacious staircase also) making it's wayup collegehill, the roadstill looking patchy from where the tramlines had been lifted ... Mo chuig ceod cumha go dubhach faoi bhron, Tu ag sileadh na sul is do chom gan lon! Nouse being hungry aswell as sad, mylove ... so she re mem ers in the future onenight when they take time out tobe to gether (he was on the afterwards train where he vowed to get her, his strength surged through his body as he thought of the moment der zug entered Mihiwaka and darkness) your hands are full of passion and they fold over mine like a baby's, she said Seotho a thoill, na goil go foill, Do gheobhair gan dearmad taisce gach seoid, nodont cry just yet my love my treasure (not his wife, not her wife) Do bhi ag do shinsear rioga ronihat (not Homburg nein) In - Eirinn iath-ghlais Choinn is Eoghaim (is what?) ... five hundred sorrows, you are crying and I lament as the train goes, stops briefly at Purakanui and Waitati, and then works and winds its way round Parimoana, the cliffs and the sea wild and changeable as the great feelings of his pass (i) on ... and as helooks out now he sees, at sundown, the talltrees on the horizon, the harbour headsand the delicate merging of colours ofindeterminate shapes, number them ... has he lost her before he ever gother, the questions of all lovers dream through his being, can their love be of this world and as hemoves through te wahi moemea i rotoi te waka ia he feels the pain and the joy of life ... theyholdhands and talk ... she avoids his eyes and his embrace is awkward, avuncular, they not yet free and they never will be, but he is happy with and doesn't receive any more than the small quantity of the esculent *matériel* of her love, because freedomisa word I rarely usewithout thinking ... Brrrrrum brrrrrum vrooomm vrroooomm if itisn't the V8 pushbike (not B4 time although originallymaybe) and ifit isn't Pita Edith (worldfamous innewzealand) one Olds thistime notan oldone as before (not B4) andhimself quiteovercome with an ocean of the thoughts (the torts to remaininside thelaw!) as his memoryglands secrete secretly ... pitaedit h looksdown on the creaturehimself and takes pity edits the latest sentence ofhimself who thensees the tripodseat on the veeeight tricycle with the stamp MAD (E) IN PARIMOANA OF ORIGIN OREGEN, PINE FOR PAST etc and him selfcan only thinkonething ... te nohoanga o te porangi ... pitaedith wholooks off ended has turnedinto Edithpiaf but b44 (and not B4) before himself can sayany thing shehe cycles off looking for the Brawl at Austerlitz or Saint Clair with a hey nonney nonney when the surfies de-eyed us as we were singinga songi of sixpence in the adult christmaspud and thehi story of the V8 called ... RING-RING PSYCLES ... and himself catches snatches ... 'smooth geared underpants raiders in '39 they tested the first VI by '43 your owners had turned to genocide gallonsof legalgas were dishedup and the V2 smashed into your stretched marks theynearly broke the deutchebanks as the riversofmoneyflowed and thepeople you degraded thought itsa goodthing thegermans neverinvented the V8, the VI andV2 werebadenbadenenough but you movedalong narrowroads dreamingof the nazisparty' ... and as the last strains of thissadreframe echoed through the snowcovered landscape himself couldnt helpthinking itstill alongway to Tipperary ... and travellin' all those Miles, noGasoline, so intothe petroltank a gallon of poteen andit wentlike abomb ifyou know what 1 mean all theway from Tipperaryto youknowwhere I mean soit stoppedjust and let the wind comein - short of St Stephensgreen and toall of thepeople who saidwhere youbeenthe drivingman replied blessed arethose whobelieveand havenot seen they're killing menandwomen for the wearingofthegreen but now I mustgo backto where I'vebeen andhe pulledout the bottleofpoteen anddrinks halfhimself sothathe eyesareagleam, thenhe pouredtherest into hismachine and all the plainpeople of Ireland cando isstare at the wonderofitall, yeti was onlyone of those anomalous practitioners in low erde partments of the law ... beep beep, burp burp, yeah ... but him selfas waspredicted issoon laughingon theother side ofhisface (myboy!) because notinthe toodistant distance he sees the twosisters riding in tandem ona tandem (daisydaisy I'm half crazy!) their seductive soft rrring rrrring rrrring is heard and his dingaling responds naturally, naturally, Munchasen is standing in the shadows of love me do - heloves andwants themboth, their broth has beensimmering on hisfire for manymoons and as they appear fromout of the darkness the snowstopsfalling and themoon againappears brightand full inthe coolrnid winter sky and as the sisters pull nearerto this neredogood both of themsilently (forthey donotspeak to oneanother) dismount (sic) and instead of obtaining a mirror, obtain a person and hecan see thepeak of the centralnorthisland mountains rising everhigher before him and as te marama (whois alsoone ofthe sisters) andher starspiked cloak spreadover him hefeels theancient volcanoes which are above himand beneath himand around him, they are also withinhim and the centuriesold lavabetween hisloins beginsto move, heisenchanted and embraced by her nakedness which is underher cloak foronly him tosee butjust as theyare aboutto reach hispeakof their lovemaking heforlornly lookson as theother sister pushes Marama to oneside of him andas theybegin a jealous and maliciousfight he, himself, sees himselfas Pihanga and the twosisters are Tongariro and Taranaki fightingover thesameman who in legendwasa woman andthey weremen andas hesees te atahua o te marama recedingfrom him to the west he sees thatshe was themother of hisdaughter (not his daughter) andhe is fullof sadness forher return buthe hasno time to think forthe victorious wahine o te Tongariro isonto him, andhe is helplessas she winds herwebb of seduction aroundhim her beautiful brownbreasts are delicately and deliciouslyabove him andhe feels her teke opening onto his fully erect raho andshe is moving inlong slow gestures herface ecstatic in the moonlight, histouch and hertouch sosensuous they both ache andcryout together andthrough his ears atsmall intervalshe hears her whisper almost inaudibly 'comein, comein' inurgent shortburstsof hervoice, and then 'letit stand' (as a tilt of the hat to the master and mistress) as the onlyunbroken partsof his bodyrespondsto her invocations hermouth hungry yetsubtle findshis, herthick firmsoft lips meet hisand theirtongues entwine asthey kissandfuck kissandfuck kissandfuck and she comesbefore hedoes in moansand groans of pleasure and release andjust as the earthshakes andhe isabout toerrupt, hiseyes closed in semiconscious sweetness of sweat and the smells of sex, again that *belle haleine, au de viollette* mixed with vanilla and woodruff fizz powder scenting the coldair, hehears brring brring and hiseyes open to seetwo sisters ridingoff ontandem, and as he sees Marama fold hercloak of stars around her hesees their daughter, Hinemoana alsodisappear, and Hine whohas come hasnow gone also, the three of them rideoff intandem as they abandon himself lying there, theone one part of hisbody left standing silhouetted against the fallingagain snow and hisbody writhes in sexualagony which hecant evenrelieve because evenhis fingers arebroken ... (itsa hard life!) ... and as the strengthof his sex ualdesire gradually dissipates heis left feeling drainedand bereft with morepain becauseof the further bruises andcuts hegot, he begat during his dreamreality of begatting, heis melancholyalso from hispost coital non coitusmetionedout andits notjust his grey which matteroffactedly oozes as he loses more as time goesby, playwith it again Hine hecalls andwishes andwants as hissperm also oozesout onto the whiteness of virginsnow but he is ofcourse alone (there is doubtwhether even mandrakes willgrow in thisclimate!) well I'll be hanged (orwell hung asit might havebeen back in 1984 old hat now, and nowhere tohangit - put it in the hangi and we'll seehowit comes out kapai te kai) and ashis manhood drainsaway sodoes hislife and hisbrain stilloozes onto this page as the paincomes inwaves comesinwaves comesinwaves lappingat thefeet of his (himselfs) existence, so that now when a room is needed, obtain a person instead of a room, but the songs from a room loom like The Future thoughts of El Cid of Elfresco and Jesu Elpifcoandipandi pain becomeone as theyreach across the sea ofhis existence from eternity, the ancestors are calling and coming, hislovers are calling and his children (not his children) are callingand coming, hisparents are calling and coming his sistersand brothers and manyothers arecallingand coming, those whohave neverbefore seen him are callingandcoming callingandcoming callingandcoming like an ancient karanga calling the mokopuna home this callingandcoming is pullingat hislife but he resists hewants to live hewants to survive hewantsto see his children (not his children) grow. Hewants warmth andcomfort and love, not these maddelusions andinsights let himwalk down the street andfeel the ground and see the coloursoflife not this black andwhite landscape of unrelenting coldness and loneliness inwhich his lifeis gradually receding even the whiskeywarmth is beginning to wane (Jeez wane whereis Jesus) as it too oozes its finite fulfullness slipping the everwidening gap he is dying throughahole inhishead ... soitseems factsmustbe faced ... thinking only keepsout the ghosts like the daykeeps out thenight ... himself hearsthe whistle of alongago train andthinks fora moment thathe mightbe saved, butagain its onlya memoryof whatused tobe tiedto a hopeof what mighthavebeen, if you knowwhat Imean, Imean Imean Imean andwhat Imeanis, andwhat himself hearis, anold song, an air floatingon the air comingacross the waves thus: again, is he arty, is he deep: does he wake, or does he sleep: hooray and up she rises early in the mourning, singing the Doxology in unison, that was their amunition, for young Willie McBride and some French moderns aka Flanders in the field swanning around like here's harry ... withpride, the knowledge of his ancestor laying 12 thousandmiles of railway inonly 10 years made himfeel fullof warmth and he almost could sense the snowandice melting around him suchwas his sensibility ... but the reality wasdifferent forboth and as the statistictrain rolled away down the line ofhistory woe woe woooe woooe he could feel the melancholy of his race with its fullweight upon ... up on himmmmm ... and anotherdrift of snow blew across the barren wasteland, hewas the stuffed man (really tired), live on him for he wasthe hollowman (hollowhollow - anybodyhome?) his headpiece wassurrounded by hoarfrost and the deep whiteness threatened to en gulf him en tire ly ... so Patrickfitzgerald stepped off the donegalrailway in eighteenfiftytwo and sailed with his nowgrowing child far ... andtheywere wellat sea (although there were manywho were not wellof course, there weresome who were welloffcourse!) when he realised he and his littleone wouldbe landingin New Zealand and not New York (what do youmean not New York!) and he just thought, hunger doesfunny things to a man (but as an afterthought, not so funnythings to a woman, as he remembered his wife like an old sackof spuds lying on the frozen Irish ground and he crydandcryd) ... things startedto slow, the lifeflow even the snow fell oneflake ata time, sweetjesus and eve ry word, eve ry thought broke up in to syl a bills fal ling down and down through his mind, through the con sci ous ness of him self and his im pond er able sit u a ti on and his im poss ib le pre dic a mant (but not sta ted) the word s be came less com pre hen sib le the (or though) hard er he tried to un der stand, he felt that his brain (ourbryanee) was a slow ly spin ning spin oze an fish tank (anunderwonderwall, by Pope George-Ringo II, and it only seems like yesterday when, whilst eating ham and eggs, Pope John-Paul III was watching Mr Boris Norris changing trains at Friedrichstrasse Station after coming home from the Hunt Ball wearing a clever mask given in supplication by Anni, when a similarly Silhouetted Head leant out one of the windows, shouting *Prosit Neujahr!* – you can just imagine the fallout!) and nev ere societ why of disc boy lik eee in snoweee rivets of cru mpie gup gup gup, hello Guppee says Sambo when he comes up-up-upee out of the water, as trang erbel ieve dubble seaing hap pap me weep on sun day mass des truction tra ction yip sno sno sno fal fal fal the wo man eyem tink ingov the lifeflow even the snow fell oneflake ata time, sweetjesus and eve ry word, eve ry thou oght broke up in to silly bus a bills fal ling down and down through his mind, while Fred tried to convey his zur = 'On' and uber = 'About' Bruno was stating it in more everyday terms like Versprechen = 'Slips of the tongue' or perhaps 'Lapse' which to Alex was as interesting as his OT routines, making designs for chessmen, but ireality they were just more MaD ideas, now turned NoMaD, they were just more thoughts that slipped through the con sci ous holes ne us of him self and his im pond er able dream together inter-pre-tit sit-ua-tion and his im poss ib le pre dic a mant (but not sta ted) the word s be cume loss com pre hen syb le the (or though) hard er he tried to kun der stand, he felt that his bain (ourbryanee) was a slow ly spint ing sprig ooze an fish tank (anunderwandawll) and nev ere societ why of disc boy lik eee in snoweee thoughts like flick er ring frozen sparks wereing or gent lyspin ning out of his nose ... bleedbut gent ly brothhergently underst andand thisslowsnow falling downwas as a

p ro cess is,oneofthe uncol lect

edthoughts and woand

 rds anddiseasescycle andepicycle   ofthemanhimselfpassed onunhinddered each word,became a heyheyhey snow flake asthesnowfelllight lyand was whirledaround andkeptfromsettlingby amo unt ainofwindwhich hadsprungupbut now itisjustas (nothereis none) jesusjester qu icklyandquietlybeg an t ofall andthesnow   andthe   WO   rds   began   flowin   gMOrefreely againsosothathimselfwasyetagain tryingtoregainto orb in orbgain respitefrom burialby   w   hitearth (not how now cow boy, not the cow!) tokeepwarmifonlyinternally,hethoughtrivetsofcru mpie hulup gup gup as trang erbel ieve dubble seaing hap pap meof you boat fame, and if onelooked close by e nough (iseoughisenough) as the ground, his thoughts coincided he thought of his wife (not hiswife) and he tried to compose the most beau tiful poem in the world to her, whichwas something he had al wayswanted todo for her, he thought and randomlines from pastpoems he had written toher sauntered through as someonestood lookingat the starlitsky dreaming, titiro ki te tonga saw the pot and scorpions tale (but didnt listen to the noise of the chuggingdiesel engine saying whakarongo mai her last words till next time my darling goodnight) whakarongomai through te po o te pari Hinemoana ... but that was someoneelse for the snowfell on himself in the measuredmetre of blankverse ... he longed to give expression to the passionhe felt forher, sometimes so strong he felt the skywould open and the universe wouldexplode through eternity but he wascalm as the words flowed, old words he wanted towear a blankmask, towrite newones but the old ones pushed out and fell through his consciousness with the samesteady consistency withwhich the snowfell ... slowlycreeping nga kupu atahua, nga kupu o te aroha, nga kupu ora, nga kupu o te mate, forward they came one by one, the words of the past, moving through the present towards the future, then to linkupagain with the past (the point of misunderstanding for the anglosaxonfuturists) ... whakarongo! we satsilent at the footof the poetsstatue ... we waited ... for the time wewould nolongerbe to gether ... myarm moved instinctively a way ... we are a part wegrowtogether ... the aroha is be tweenus as well as the dis tance ... thebestthing was we were happy ... we laughed and danced sang ... and talked of death and darkness and light ... to sitsilent at the foot of the poets statue ... kia aroha, kia kaha e wahine toa! ... one thousand miles is not a long distance for dreams to travel, unravel as the mystery grows ... the evil and the joy of the world are within all of us ... storms of destruction and devastation standalong side the beauty of the sky meeting the sea at the horizon, the gently blowing wind scattering the small whispyclouds, the headland juts out its ancient form and manyvarieties of trees transform the latewinter landscape with their colours and shapes reaching upandout wards, the sea seems lifted above the land, reaching and meeting the heavens half way as that wideboy the sagacious Delboeuf sees and declares 'intellegence, imagination, memory, will and morality remain essentially intact, but a dreamer is an actor who at his own will plays the parts of madmen and philosophers, of executioners and their victims, of dwarfs and giants, of demons and angels' and the Donkey's descent into the wild Emerald Hell where absinthe makes the head no longer strong ... in fact he and she were like limbo lovers, neither here nor there ...

LSD flash-back, circa early 1970s: when I was young it was more …

'Not a very interesting life, is it?' said Paul Te Ariki, slipping on his old and tattered silk dressing gown. Patrick Mika pondered the statement, rolling it around in his mind like brandy in a barrel.

'And I'm a pretty boring sort of fellow, all my life I've tried to put it from me,' he thought to himself. Paul Te Ariki watched the slow, imbecilic grin grow, bloom and wilt and thought 'Skin two thousand balloons, Trev, it wasn't that funny!' Paul Te Ariki was always irritable this early in the morning and the least trifle could upset his equilibrium at five minute intervals for the following two hours.

Today was their big day. They both had one big day a week which was, without fail, the same day for both of them. It was a day which neither could do without and it produced such traumatic and extreme behaviour in them, both physical and psychological (the spiritual realm shall not be dealt with in this treatise as it is equally abhorrent to both protagonists, and as their biographer I feel as though I would be held responsible for resultant reprisals on the reader – I should then be found guilty by a public court which would make the trial of Heinrich Himmler seem like one for petty theft, or as they say in classical theatre, *Sine Cerere*) that all their friends knew to keep well away until the midnight celebration which was held at the end of every such day, and ask them to write a will to you before boarding if they survived, which they always had so far.

'It's eleven o'clock and here is the news. Today President Sadat ... 'Had an erection!' Paul Te Ariki's voice blended in with that of the news reader's so convincingly that Patrick Mika who had spent the last quarter of an hour on a philosophical problem encountered whilst tying up his shoe-laces, suddenly leapt to his legs and in a resounding jubilant baritone said 'Did you hear that'.

Paul Te Ariki gave him a quick furtive glance and grimaced as he answered, 'What's up!' to Patrick Mika. 'Sadat's had an erection! It said so on the news! Didn't you hear it! Mandrax grows when it falls.'

'How?' Paul Te Ariki said, with a sense of subdued glee, being careful not to look his friend in the eye.

'What do you mean how? In the usual way, I imagine! They didn't say. He probably thought justly that the most upright judge would know.'

'He no doubt brought himself to it – all Arabs are a pack of wankers' said Paul Te Ariki, with a Jewish bent, beginning to laugh openly now.

 'Anyway, continued Patrick Mika excitedly, 'that's not the point. What I'm taken by is that they actually said it on the radio, - Erection!' Patrick Mika had become quiet – almost abstract … 'Erection, they said erection on the programme and shortwaves service of Radio New Zealand, National. It's too much for one man.'

He was staring off into space for several minutes while Paul Te Ariki was rolling on the floor with tears of laughter streaming down his young face. After a while his reality forced itself into Patrick Mika's trance-like state by its sheer physical weight of sound. Patrick Mika looked at his friend with disgust. 'Puerile, vile creature, no sense of guilt or culture,' he muttered to himself, and turning away had a sudden retinal encounter with the clock on the mantlepiece and gave a start.

'Holy Christ, saviour of the world and other planets, it's 11.15 a.m. Make a key quickly, and find a lock that fits. If we don't hurry we will miss the bus and thus our appointments with the esteemed Labour Department and out lives will be in ruin.'

'Pus!' hissed Paul Te Ariki who had picked up the heap of rubble, which was himself, off the floor. Both men looked at each other, and all antipathy vanished as they realised they had to once more cope with their common problem. This brought each of them to a state of frigidity no woman could match, oh, youthful benefactress! They stood frozen, both felt as though they were made of wood which had been left in the refrigerator for some suburban family's pet termite; they were AP-PALLED, that is, terror had struck!

No need to explain all the nuances involved in their malaise. Suffice it to say that when either or both decided to go out of their dwelling on their own accord or were forced out by some form of coercion such as the present, they were seized by a terrible and unaccountable fear, which was simply this: neither knew when they stepped outside into the repulsive rays of sunlight which distinguished day from night, whether they would be stepping into the streets of Auckland or the streets of Dunedin.

Were they in Ponsonby or Normanby; were they in Herne Bay or St Clair. Were they in Karangahape Road or George Street; were they in Symonds Street or Princess Street; Anzac Avenue or Anzac Avenue ... their dilemma intensified as the seconds rushed by and their bus drew nearer to the stop at which they alighted. Their appointment was at 12.30 p.m., their bus left at 11.45 a.m. This left exactly one quarter of an hour to dress, shave, wash and run. So, as usual, they did. They burst from inside to outside, slammed the door and then raced the bus in the hundred metres dash to the bus stop.

Although the vehicle was of the vintage trolley-bus era it managed to beat its human vintage counter-parts and it was only the usual chance that someone was already waiting at the stop which made it possible for the degenerate duo to leap on to the conveyance just as it was leaving. Patrick Mika was the first on board, thus avoiding the humiliation and embarrassment which would follow as soon as Paul Te Ariki would get on. The torture which follows the total blank experienced in the mind which follows the hapless words ... 'I would like two to' ... Two to where? To the exchange or the Civic Centre; two to the Octagon or to Customs Street; two to High Street or to High Street ... 'Where to?' repeated the driver, becoming somewhat irate (every sperm is sacred) at the dumbfounded expressions on the faces of his two passengers. Suddenly Patrick Mika's face lit up like the firmament and he pulled eighty cents from his pocket, handed it to the astounded driver and said in an extremely confident audible voice, 'Two to the city!'

An unsolicited e-mail from poetry.com

suddenly popped up like a pop-up on the screen of the scene: YOU SHOULD HAVE BEEN A POET There is great news and I want to be the first person to tell you. You are nominated for this year's Poet of the Year competition. It was not hard at all choosing this year's nominees, just prescribe pills for going through the wall and have only the hair come back, because your talent and dedication to poetry make you an obvious choice. We want you to share this momentous occasion with us in Las Vegas, Nevada, July 19-22, 2007 for the 21st Annual International Society of Poets Convention and Symposium. We are just now putting the finishing touches on what is sure to be the biggest poetry celebration of the decade, books with a Japanese influence, no Joko. Why? Just look!

Songs of a Tokio Greengrocer
i
 Tokio Central
A bullet train fires, mushroom
Crowd, Hiroshadow
ii
Alles verfallen
Axis old as love, pasta
Melon, cauli, fish
iii
Ginza, people walk
Everywhere, street lanterns ignite
My vegetables
iv
Don't assume Basho
Azuma Bashi Poets
Free delivery
v
Seed of Edo grow
After Kyoto reclaim
Tall trees scrape skywards
vi
Orders tomatoes
But streets have no names, so Yu
Tu gets potatoes
vii
Ticket gets you there
Chikatetsu – walkway
Or apples and pears
viii
Amidst Aoyama
And Ikebukuro lies
The real city, small
ix
Diet library
Rice paper, turn lettuce leaves
Look, Sushi cook book!
x
Hana Kawado
And her sisters, Senso Ji,
Asakusa peach
xi
Nartia welcome!
From Hameda visit friends
Take a fresh cabbage

LSD flash-back, circa early 1970s: when I was young it was more ...

Hinemoana strolled leisurely down the road which led from her home to the railway station, observing as seeing a slow motion film. She had at least ten minutes to walk the final hundred yards or so and it was a beautiful spring afternoon. All the gardens (looks to me more like a bush) of suburban Johnsonville had a bright colourful atmosphere despite the dreary mentality of the people who had laid them. The train had not yet arrived at the Johnsonville Station as she crossed the tracks and walked along the platform.

There were not many people waiting to catch the unit back to Wellington: a few shift workers from the state-housing areas who would go into Wellington and wait for another train to take them to some god-forsaken factory up the Hutt Valley. Hinemoana mused, almost brooded, on this point. She was thinking what hard lives some people must have when the train arrived and broke her whimsical contemplation, thinking of what the next person is thinking.

'Good afternoon, Hinemoana,' said Mr Johnson, as he stepped on the platform to the music of one of those airs played on a barrel-organ.

'Oh! Good afternoon, Mr Johnson. Have you had a good day?' said Hinemoana as she realised where she was.

'Nothing too strenuous,' replied Mr Johnson, 'and where are you off to?' Hinemoana looked at her next-door neighbour with an air of disbelief and then said quickly,

'I'm going to visit a friend in another part of the country. I'll be away for a few days, he said Saturday, I think, so I've fixed up with Mrs Johnson to feed the cats.'

'Fine,' replied Mr Johnson. 'Good-by; and have a good trip.'

'Thank you, I will', she said.

Hinemoana watched Mr Johnson, with affectionate amusement as he walked slowly down the platform, and his dark, well-pressed suit, his bowler hat, and his umbrella reminded her of Paul Te Ariki's first reaction to her aged penguin-like friend. He had been staying with her whilst in transit between Auckland and Dunedin or vice-versa (she could never remember which) and after he had been introduced to her neighbour he sat down later that evening and wrote a very funny, satirical short story which he called: '*Johnson of Johnsonville*: a definitive history of a civil servant with a past I don't understand.'

As Hinemoana boarded the 3.15 p.m. train she remembered her mock-anger as she chastised Paul Te Ariki for making fun of such a lovely old man. Paul Te Ariki had taken an amoral stance, change your name by the period of your age, qua Riccardo, and the story was so good and he was so beautiful and incorrigible that she had to forgive him his follies. As the train pulled away from the station she gave a sudden start. Her feelings were at once excited and apprehensive. She had not seen Paul Te Ariki for nearly two months and she could not help keep wondering if he had changed and how, and how they would react to each other.

They had been together for nearly two years and had broken up at the beginning of the year because he did not want to move to Wellington. She had moved there because of her job with television and apart from that one time when he had stayed for a week during transit between the two poles which governed his existence, they had not seen each other for eight or nine months. As the train left

Ngaio Station Hinemoana looked once more at the telegram which had arrived shortly after 2.30 p.m.

'Hinemoana, dear. We both received a large sum of back-pay from the dole office about half-an-hour ago and are having a party tonight. Go to airport and pick up your ticket before 6.30 p.m. It is paid for stop./Go./The plane leaves Wello at 7p.m./stop. We had better stop here/stop/as this telegram has already cost over a thousand dollars, no mode of sufficiently speedy of obtaining money than this has ever occurred to us calm ... calm, the English say cawm ... stop/stop/stop/

Love Patrick Mika and Paul Te Ariki.'

Hinemoana laughed aloud and the few other passengers looked at her and then looked quickly away as she turned and realised where she was. She felt embarrassed despite herself and was annnoyed that she could not enjoy herself openly in public. 'What a pack of morons' she thought harshly and then she felt remorse for thinking so badly of others, as though she had received her letters from Mick Jagger, the Earl of Altamont and his Angels frm Hell. She brought this line of thought to a close by saying to herself, 'Paul Te Ariki is right! I am just an ordinary New Zealander with all the resultant hang-ups!' She felt both bemused and sad at this thought and to avoid thinking anymore at the moment she turned and looked out of the window of the train.

The train had just emerged from the last tunnel on the line and was now clanking over the viaduct which took it across the worm-like motorway which was gradually eating its way through the core of the capital city. Hinemoana had caught a glimpse of Oriental Bay and the surrounding hills on which the late afternoon sun shone harsh and oblique. Wellington seemed hard-edged and gold-tinted on one side and dark, sumptuous and sombre on the other and Hinemoana thought of a golden Inca temple-city which had been liberated from hundreds of years of rubble – half beauty and half decay.

The train was now entwined in a mass of rails and points, lights of green, red, and amber shone at the places where rails ran into one another. As the unit pulled into Wellington Central Railway Station, Hinemoana could see the people on the outside waiting with tired, anxious faces and weary, sagging bodies burdened down with parcels, satchels, and all manner of paraphernalia, just dying to get into their mobile cocoons which would then whisk them homeward, getting home when it is dark. Hinemoana always felt guilty because she had a job which allowed her to take time off whenever she wanted, was well-paid and interesting. As she got out of her carriage she thought, 'One day I'll get a 'real' job,' and then, 'Only joking' and crossed her fingers, let's wait and see what Munchausen says:

To slacken virtue, and abate her edge
Than tempt her to do aught may merit praise

It was 6.05 p.m. by the time the bus reached the airport terminus. Between getting off the train or on the bus, Hinemoana had been to say goodby to Cherryl and was feeling really good. She walked straight up to the ticket counter and collected her ticket. She then sat down, lit a cigarette and read he newspaper until her flight number was called.

She was in the middle of an article on the future of the Middle-East when a woman's voice called over the speaker. 'Attention! Attention! Flight 614 for

Auckland and Flight 710 for Dunedin. All aboard please. Passengers for Flight 614 go through gate 2 and for Flight 710 through gate 4. Thank you.'

Hinemoana put her newspaper in her bag and stood up. She was motionless in thought for a few seconds and then walked off quickly through the gate to her plane.

An unsolicited e-mail from poetry.com

suddenly popped up like a pop-up on the screen of the scene: YOUR WORSHIP WISHES TO ASSERT HIS PREROGATIVES?

There is great news and I want to be the first person to tell you. You are nominated for this year's Poet of the Year competition. It was not hard at all choosing this year's nominees. Your talent and dedication to poetry make you an obvious choice. We want you to share this momentous occasion with us in Las Vegas, Nevada, July 19-22, 2007 for the 21st Annual International Society of Poets Convention and Symposium, and to talk about the death of an imaginary person. We are just now putting the finishing touches on what is sure to be the biggest poetry celebration of the decade.

Doomsblay:

(One Hundred Years of Desmond and Molly, Ha, Ha Ha Ha)
Everything seemed exact, yet dislocated
The old Stock Exchange building standing
In pre-neon illuminated clock flashed
An iridescent flicker onto the tramlines

The streets looked washed and clean
As after pre-Hendrix summer rain
The time flashed again – Kuata pahi
Ono karaka – followed by the date

It was their first walk together
As the 6.15 tram to Caversham
Went clanking past they saw ti-ed?
16th June, 1904, written in the sky

Te tekau ma ono o nga ra o Hune;
Ko te kau kotahi mano iwa rau ma wha
Day of Days, Holies of Holies
Heaven and Earth are full of your glory

They planned a coach ride to Sandymount
'Next Tuesday – it's only 1s/6d each way,'
Hinengaro and Patrick Mika were in love
As James and Nora, in their own way

Doomsblay maybe amidst the smoke of battle,
But there is no battle in the smoke of Juno
Wai Rongoa now holds ten special gold medals
As they walked quickly past Dallas and Watts

All along the Boulevard de Dunedineaux
It was getting dark now and the last tram
Up the valley would soon be leaving, that waka
Entering into the strange seas of moemoeä

From the rising cloud of a locomotive's boiler
A moko also appeared engraved on its surface
This Moko told an ancient story of Abelard
And his niece and their ill-fated love

Just like Romeo and Hinemoanat, to raise
One hand with Hinemoa and Tutanekai
Kei te kata nei ano, kua mane te ngakau
A, te mutunga o taua koa he pouri ...
The cloud face, smiling down at them
Leading them closer towards the cliffs
And they were falling, falling down
All the days from 1904, down the thousand
Miles from Tamaki ma kaurau to Otepoti
– its still the same old story ...

LSD flash-back, circa early 1970s: when I was young it was more ...
Patrick Mika and Paul Te Ariki leapt off the trolley-bus and headed home. They
looked like two large bats as they sped along the footpath – their movements
were filled with a sense of urgency, their long black coats flying out like capes.
They walked with their eyes downwards in order to avoid seeing the street
names which stuck out so tantalisingly from what seemed like each lamp-post,
the essential doesn't change.
The reason they so religiously ignored, what might seem to an outsider, the most
obvious and immediate solution to their twin-city schizophrenic problem was that
they had tried it once and it had created more chaos than ever. Indeed, you
might say it created such ghastly phantoms as ever haunted the couch of an
Orestes. It was during the particularly cold winter of 1972 when they both refused
to go abroad even to the local dairy. The telephone and Hinemoana were their
only communication with the outside world and it was through these media that
all provisions, needs and wants were attended to. For fun they would take one
mannerism from one kind of animal and make it theirs for a week.
In July or August of 1974 ... they had become so intent on finding out which city
they were in that it had become an obsession. So one day they sent Hinemoana
out to solve once and for all this hitherto insoluble dilemma. She was sensible
and could no doubt conclude the matter one way or the other. Hinemoana went
to the corner store and brought a newspaper. On her way home a light snow
shower fell. Not being able to wait until the snow falls further she ran, reaching
home almost in an ecstasy, burst through the door, threw the paper on the floor
and, after catching her breath told Paul Te Ariki and Patrick Mika of the snow.
Patrick Mika cried,
'We must be in Dunedin!'

Paul Te Ariki was about to give Patrick Mika a triumphant embrace (both had agreed from the start that their relationship would have the barest amount of physical contact, reserved for special occasions when they triumphed over the world together. For, although the loved the 'poetic element' in each other, they both repulsed each other physically, in the extreme) when his wayward glance happened upon the headlines of the newspaper which lay open at the front page by his feet.

Paul Te Ariki, with a sharp gesture, repulsed his friend's open arms, 'Let me go!' and fell, moaning like a sick animal, to the couch. Patrick Mika, at first taken aback, then much alarmed, looked at Hinemoana for an insight into what he should do. She went over to Paul Te Ariki and asked him what was wrong. Both she and Patrick Mika had no trouble in comprehending what had sent their friend into such anguish after Paul Te Ariki had pointed them towards the headlines of the paper. It was not the large type which read 'Coldest winter in New Zealand's history' that took the tongues out of their heads but a smaller headline ... 'Snow falls on Ponsonby: first time for fifty years.'

Hinemoana went over to Paul Te Ariki and slowly nursed him back to a state in which he was anything but *ponderibus librata suis*, however, his wits were such as to be able to see the door slam behind Patrick Mika.

'Where's he going?' Paul Te Ariki shouted. He brooded briefly, thinking where his friend might have gone.

'Patrick Mika has not been outside for two or three months' he thought. 'He could come to grief.' Suddenly he turned panic-stricken to Hinemoana and screamed ...

'He's imitating Oliver Reed. Oh! My God!' and an image of Patrick Mika wandering off alone to his death in the snows of Mount Cargill or One Tree Hill or wherever the fucking hell they were flashed across his unbalanced mind. He lay motionless: impotent and listless he mumbled things to himself: inaudible noises which Hinemoana could not decipher. 'Count all the words in this book instead of reading them,' he seemed to say. Sweat poured off his bumpy forehead as he remembered the brief oblivion of *Wrongs unredress'd, and insults unavenged.*

Patrick Mika wandered through the decaying part of the city past derelict houses and disused shops and factories, after all, the road is free to all. It was a small area in relation to the greater area of the city but it was the part he knew and loved. He had few human attachments, so his emotional outlets were satisfied in the main by the parts of Dunedin and Auckland which had long ago been deserted by decent folk. The parts where the students, migrant workers, and poorer natives lived, or else those which the authorities had ear-marked for urban renewal in more affluent times, and could now not even afford to demolish let alone rebuild.

There was a slight snow falling, mixed with drizzle and night was descending like a large dark velvet curtain. Lights were being turned on everywhere and the whole atmosphere appeared to Patrick Mika like a surrealistic pillow-field of mushrooms springing up to meet the night. However, on this occasion his mission was stronger than his melancholia. He was going to look at street names and he would do this by seeking out likely lamp-posts as a dog might.

The difference between him and his canine counterpart would be simple and unambiguous. Whereas a dog would surely tilt a back leg to 45° angle on making the desired encounter, he would tilt his head on the angle of 45° in order to read the street and thus solve the mystery previously mentioned. In other words 'more verbs than adjectives,' but, there could be even other words than these.

'Such is the sublime difference between man and beast' mused Patrick Mika. Then turning to his business he wandered on, head down, deep in thought. He walked for about a mile, past many lamp-posts. He was so absorbed in preoccupation he forgot to make the necessary angular tilt. In his mind he was trying to collate all the information his brain had stored on the subject he had asked it about which was!

'Could you please tell me, my little mind, the names of the streets in Auckland from roughly the area border by Karangahape Road, Ponsonby Road, College Hill and Queen Street which correlate with the street names in Dunedin found in the area roughly bordered by Stuart Street, Anzac Avenue, Dundas Street, Duke Street and Queen Street.'

Soon the answers flowed in, and Patrick Mika thought, 'Before I venture any further, if I can find out all the streets of the same nomenclature in the two areas, when I finally come to street with a different name all I have to do is see which city it's in, and I will have a certain knowledge of where we are in. He became progressively excited as the street names flowed from his brain. Smith, Brown, Howe, Russell, Scotland, Union, London, Pitt, Harbour, Queen.

As the definite flow came to a halt Patrick Mika found himself leaning against a lamp-post at the corner of the street in case he fold certain parts of a paper and read, oh me; oh my. Here he forgot the dishonours of the grave and thought only of the keys to paradise, that just, subtle, and mighty LSD. Beads of sweat had settled on his brow. He knew the moment of truth had come. The age of reason had been reached and he must live with and use the knowledge he was about to receive. He became calm and without further hesitation he took two steps away from the pole and prepared for the upward tilt which would free him from bondage.

His initial inclination had been to carry out the necessary movement of the cranium case as quickly as possible, thus enabling him to find out the street name, then deduce the identity of their particular whereabouts all in a matter of seconds. However, the significance of the event was so overwhelming, he thought not only was it impossible for his blood pressure to cope with such enlightenment, but also that some sense of style might be considered by so civilized a patron of the earth as himself.

The odyssey began! Head tilted 45° South up and the first letter appeared before him. M. He moved on to the next with cautious confidence, as an infant takes its second step. A. These were definitely new letters. Neither had been mentioned in conjunction with the other in the cor-relative list. Third letter, C. had his mind racing. Almost convinced of victory he read the fourth letter almost carelessly, as the fresh air stimulates the jaded appetite. K. He was now convinced! It must be MacKelvie Street, Grey Lynn. So sure was he of his vision he almost forgot to stay and read the remaining letters. He paused briefly to collect his happily scattered thoughts; onward he thought, with conviction. The next letter was E and for poor Patrick Mika it may have been a machine-gun held two inched from his head. He could not, of course, go on now, his eyes goggling out of his head.

His remembrance of a street called Mackenzie not far from the botanical gardens in Dunedin North made the situation beyond his powers of redemption. Blinded by confusion he ran reaching Paul Te Ariki and Hinemoana and their home, shattered. Both he and Paul Te Ariki thenceforth agreed to study lamp-posts as a means of solving their precise and tormenting problem. 'It seems as though the attempted solution is ten times worse than the projected disease' said Paul Te Ariki later that evening, and the incident was never talked of again, but left to fester and rot malignantly in both their minds.

Paul Te Ariki shuddered violently as he was brought back to the present by Patrick Mika's voice asking if he had the key.

'What??? Oh yes! The key! Yes I do have the key, the good old key,' he said, assuming an air of abandonment as he tried to forget the memories he had so unwittingly been engrossed in during their mad dash for home. However, Paul Te Ariki remained so distracted that when a telegram arrived about 7.30 p.m. saying 'Arriving tonight about 9.30 Love Hinemoana' he became alarmed and immediately asked a puzzled Patrick Mika his views on why she might be coming. Patrick Mika threw his arms in the air as a gesture of despair-cum-disdain, made himself a cup from the eternal painted teapot, eternal *à parte ante* and *à parte post* then went off to the bedroom for a rest.

Patrick Mika moved quickly along the narrow canyon, walked in by shops that was Karangahape Road. It was a late shopping night and people were rushing with baskets and children. Patrick Mika did not look anyone in the eye for fear of giving away his secret: select an amount of dollar, hey Judas. When he reached St Kevin's Arcade he stood for a few seconds at the corner, to check if he was being followed. He looked up and down the long, snake-like road.

On each corner an S.S. guard stood, their black demonic uniforms stood out against the well-lit streets and colourful clothes of the Polynesian people. Karangahape Road was a world unto itself and could still appear as though it were mid-day even though it may be midnight. Even the Nazi occupation had not out a damper on this festival of colour and light!

Taking a last glance Patrick Mika satisfied himself that all was in order and took a head-long dive down the steps which led to Myers Park. At the bottom of these steps in the Arcade he cam to a door on his right. No. 4 was the flat he wanted. He gave the secret knock, and with a certain amount of suspicion the old Jew at the entrance let him past and locked the door behind him, but in theory the bones go to the carrier.

The room he was led into was smoke-filled and dimly-lit. There were about thirty or forty Jewish men and women. A meeting was in progress and much emotional language was used, and many people were crying or slightly sobbing. The old man who had let Patrick Mika in raised his hand and once everyone had become silent indicated to Patrick Mika that he should speak.

Patrick Mika moved to the centre of the room and in a low, hesitant voice said, 'They've arrested Paul Te Ariki.' Everyone was stunned and stared in disbelief at this stranger who bore them such devastating news. After a while a tall man with a long beard and Jewish priest's hat came forward and said to Patrick Mika,

'I have seen you before, but many here have not. Perhaps you could explain your friendship with Paul Te Ariki and how you know of his fate. Record things happened to you in result of that.'

Patrick Mika was about to speak when there was a loud banging on the outside door. All the Jewish inhabitants of the room froze. Before they had time to panic or act the door was broken down and the room was filled with the black-death plague of twenty-five S.S. men, *who by earthly nature the effect had been wrought upon the dark materials of these Storm Troopers*. Everyone was rounded up and pushed against the far wall of the room. The soldiers formed a line of a firing squad and raised their machine-guns in preparation to shoot.

Five minutes passed and the hostages were in a prolonged state of terror and confusion: each wondered why they were still alive. Patrick Mika felt singularly odd. He had never been in the front-line of a firing squad before. He was thinking about Paul Te Ariki and the events of the day when his thoughts were interrupted by the entry of Gala Day.

Refrain: *Mundo paparazzi mi amore chicka ferdy, para sol*

Obergruppenfuerher Gala Day was an altogether strange and bizarre character. Instead of the usual black S.S. uniform he wore a pure white one. This was covered by insignia, medals and embroidery of many bright colours, yellow, red, blue, and green. He looked like the personification of a spring garden on a sunny day. He gave a cynical smile as he said,

'Guten Tag, Mein Juden Freund'. Patrick Mika looked at the person who was known as 'the laughing butcher' and remembered with self-hatred the deal he had contracted in order to save Paul Te Ariki's life. Gala Day walked over to him and said:

'Hello my friend, you have done well' and with a sharp gesture to one of the guards at the door a badly beaten body was thrown into the middle of the room. Herr Gala Day continued, a cruel smile on his handsome face.

'However, I am impertinent. As you can see, due to our very strict theories on race we could not let even one Jew live. Unfortunately, there is no such things as rehabilitation of the blood. Put one memory into one half of your head and watch the transition of that damned crocodile, and the other unutterable monsters and abortions of my dreams!' Gala Day turned to his S.S. soldiers and said, 'FIRE!'

After ten minutes of fanatical machine-gun fire, all the people lay in each other's blood but Patrick Mika was still alive. Sent into an ocean of remorse he was screaming as Gala Day and his men left saying: 'From the meanest creature one departs wiser!' Patrick Mika screamed - 'Shoot me!' He was on his knees shaking violently 'Shoot me! Shoot me!'

Patrick Mika finally heard Paul Te Ariki yelling:

'Wake up! Wake up! I haven't got a gun,' and felt Paul Te Ariki shaking him, even though they normally don't touch each other. Patrick Mika took a while to recognise the familiar surroundings of their room. When he was back to reality he was told by his friend that it was just after 9 p.m. and they still had quite a lot to do to organise for the party. Patrick Mika explained to Paul Te Ariki that he had another Nazi dream. Paul Te Ariki grimaced and asked him, 'What were you this time: a Nazi or a Jew?'

An unsolicited e-mail from poetry.com

suddenly popped up like a pop-up on the screen of the scene:

There is great news and I want to be the first person to tell you. You are nominated for this year's Poet of the Year competition. It was not hard at all choosing this year's nominees. Your talent and dedication to poetry make you an obvious choice. We want you to share this momentous occasion with us in Las Vegas, Nevada, July 19-22, 2007 for the 21st Annual International Society of Poets Convention and Hog Symposium. We are just now putting the finishing touches on what is sure to be the biggest poetry celebration of the decade. Say the word and you'll be free:

it's the word I'm thinking of
and the only word is aroha
the earth is sleeping
dreams are walking around, entering
each heart, each body
each soul is enchanted either by dreams
or nightmares haunting the darkness
with ever greater darkness
te ua, te ua, nga roimata ahau
te haunui o te wairua
te ariki kia aroha o te ao
and in the beginning was the word ...
... or as another poet once said:
Wanders Nachtlied
Über allen Gipfeln
Ist Ruh,
In allen Wipfeln
Spürest du
Kaum einen Hauch;
Die Vögelein schweigen im Walde
Warte nur, balde
Ruhest du auch

LSD flash-back, circa early 1970s: when I was young it was more ...

After spending about half an hour trying to avoid talking to a young businessman sitting next to her in the plane, Hinemoana finally succeeded and she looked out the window and fell deep into thought. She did not like travelling by air, because she usually met creeps of businessmen thinking they were Atlas, son of Jupiter, who always tried to chat her up and also she could never believe or comprehend a journey which took about 12 or 15 hours by rail or road could be made in an hour.

Also the height at which these aircraft flew made her feel vulnerable. She couldn't understand why she could survive so far from the earth whilst travelling at such a speed. It was like trying to think of God, or death, or achieve Simone's equilibrium, one could rationalise for so long then leave the rest to chance.

She tried to think of things or problems which were more tangible and more readily resolved. Paul Te Ariki was the first and most complex in the hierarchy of this lower category of thoughts. Hinemoana mused that he was like a bridge between thinking about the mystery of the blessed Virgin and what one was going to have for dinner, even if that included the gratification of witnessing the splendours of a right-royal party.

Patrick Mika inevitably occurred to her simultaneously as Paul Te Ariki came into her mind. She had known Patrick Mika first and had gone out with him quite a few times. They used to talk a lot together and were very close in a 'mystical' way. He understood a lot about people and especially women. This meant he had a lot of close female friends but never had girl friends or lovers. At the time

Hinemoana met Paul Te Ariki (he and Patrick Mika who had known each other for quite a while, were as close as two male friends could be) she and Patrick Mika had almost reached an agreement to become unofficially engaged.

One night she and Patrick Mika were around at his place and he mentioned that one of his friends from the North Island was coming to stay with him in Dunedin for about a week. That night Paul Te Ariki arrived off the railcar from Christchurch and when he and Hinemoana met the next day both knew that something immediate and irrevocable had happened inside each of them. They kept their meetings secret for about a week but Patrick Mika was aware that something was afoot and pressed the point one evening. The three of them got into a fierce argument which ended in Patrick Mika putting his coat and hat on and leaving.

They didn't see or hear from him until they received a telegram from Auckland a week later sating. 'Join me in the big A when possible. All is forgiven, invite only dead people, you waagerrims. Love. Patrick Mika.'

'Would you like a sweet to chew on, we will be landing soon,' said the hostess, as she passed a large tray of assorted lollies across the young businessman towards Hinemoana.

'Uh? Oh! I'm sorry I was away in a dream' said Hinemoana. 'Yes. I'd love one please?'

'Not too long now' said her boringly well-groomed neighbour, in a manner which she had become well aquainted with as the touch of the velvet hand like a lizard on an aeroplane and she had difficulty in avoiding so monstrous an indecorum as yawning.

'No? How long exactly?' She asked politely, almost thankful for a small dose of trivia to take her away from her own dark-edge thoughts.

'About five minutes' he replied eagerly, pleased at this sudden revival of communication with his attractive fellow-traveller. However, his pleasure was short-lived, for as he turned to resume his former intimacy, he found her in the abstracted attitude which she had been in for the previous twenty minutes, that is, taking notes about many different walls of sound, for example, p.s. to know him is to love and be murdered by him, STINYC.

Hinemoana went through a wide variety of feelings including guilt, adventure, remorse, and jealousy. Whenever she thought of either Paul Te Ariki or Patrick Mika, and there was no time when she thought of them more often or more intensely than just before she was due to see either or both of them again. 'In an hour or so I will be with them' she thought amidst feelings of anxiety, joy and anticipation. 'Oh how much I still love Paul Te Ariki' she almost talked aloud, but her thoughts were interrupted by the loud speaker.

'This is your captain speaking. We are now approaching ...' when she heard the word her heart stood still. She couldn't believe her ears!

She didn't know what to do! She fumbled in her bag for her ticket. Perhaps she had heard the man's voice wrongly. 'Yes. That's it, I wasn't listening properly.' Her reprieve however, was short-lived. One glance at the destination confirmed her fears. 'Those stupid bastards, those fucking Knooks!' she muttered angrily to herself.

'What?' enquired the young man.

'Nothing!' she retorted in such a manner as to leave no doubt that their communication was terminated.

As the jet taxied to a standstill Hinemoana felt suddenly exhausted and exasperated. She gathered her things indifferently and passed the smiling stewardess who was saying, 'I hope you had a pleasant journey,' as though she didn't exist. By the time she reached the terminal buildings she was feeling slightly more composed and realised that she had to find a telephone. Firstly she would send those two bloody idiots a telegram to say she couldn't make it to the party because they had given her a fucking ticket that sent her four fucking hundred or so miles in the wrong fucking direction: secondly she would have to ring friends in the city to see of she could stay he night.

An unsolicited e-mail from poetry.com
suddenly popped up like a pop-up on the screen of the scene:
Since launching Poets Choice: Rate My Poem, we have had a tremendous response. We have given away over 45 iPod Shuffles and $4,000.00 in cash. Use all existing armaments as decorative objects and accessories, i.e. use cannons and fighters for garden sculptures, bullets and earrings. We are committed to continuing this fun and exciting contest, and we need your help! Do I look like a man that can be made to suffer? Frankly?

Make Love and War
i
The last train is about to leave
In fact, has left ...
The cradle of Western Civilization
Is under siege
As the Euphrates burns, a river of flames
Set alight this past decade
By the twin towers of a double burning bush
The new manifestation of Western Civilization
Is engulfing and eating its own parents
USA, teenager of the world
New kid on the old block
With raging hormones of revenge ...
The last train has pulled out
From the stations of My Lai and Fallujah and Lidice
It doesn't matter who's killing ya
If you're being killed
Talking to someone who fought in Vietnam
Who witnessed the murder of women and children
He claims the SS troops were more honest
Than the Black Hawks up ...
(I've lost my K & P, so you must learn
do not use ready-made objects to burn – MaD)
There being no suggestion in this war which is lost
Of a triumphial return led by a crusading host

ii
My love comes to me
And baring her beautiful breasts

Before my loving gaze
And soft caress
She gives me the gift
Only a young woman
Can bestow on an older man ...
The strange healing, and holding up of a mirror
The touch of the goddess ...
And no matter how humble
His or her beginnings have been
That gift of love, of aroha
Although tainted by temporal concerns
Cannot be lost, as the flow
Of life loosens itself
From its strictures ...
iii
The doors after perception, open
As does the grave
The tomb beckons to ...
The hikoi of Hope (*all three look at the sky*)
The procession of Enough
The long line to the Unknown Soldier
Wending its way through the Wellington streets
Like a river of remembrance ...
When its all over
The soldiers remind me of death
My young love's breasts remind me of love
Now she is gone
And who will say
'Did you miss me?'

LSD flash-back, circa early 1970s: when I was young it was more ...
'I wonder where Hinemoana's got to' said Patrick Mika, 'her flight got in about
two hours ago.' Paul Te Ariki was talking with the first arrivals at the party and
didn't hear Patrick Mika's words, only his voice select a subject.
'What?' said Paul Te Ariki. Before Patrick Mika could repeat himself he was
distracted by a knock at the door.
'I'll get it.' He said, thinking to himself that it was rather odd, 'People don't knock
on the door they just open it,' and 'too early for the police' he mused as he
opened the door.
'Paul Te Ariki!' he called anxiously, 'a telegram'
Paul Te Ariki broke off from his friends and hurried over to the door.
'Well open it! Quickly!' he shouted. Patrick Mika clumsily pulled at the envelope.
'Don't rip it!' said Paul Te Ariki frantically, any hint of danger triggered off
immediate panic reactions in both of them which increased ten-fold as each
second passed, in memorium, *the bloody writing by all nations torn*. Both read
the message.
'Dear fools stop. You may use a letter or a diary instead of a mirror stop. You
have sent me to the wrong city stop by accident and incompetence I hope stop I
will be staying at Joan's in Union Street stop Reluctant Love Hinemoana.'

Patrick Mika and Paul Te Ariki looked at each other embarrassedly, went white in the faces, were silent and stood for about two minutes, looked at the walls, floor and ceiling, and finally looked each other directly in the eye again and simultaneously burst into a fit of uncontrollable laughter. This was their usual response to any emotional trauma whether it be suspension from the dole or the death of a friend.

After a while they reached a state of elegant equilibrium and thus resumed their roles as hosts, seemingly purged, by a complex system of well-rehearsed hysterics, we don't know what our twilights can do, of the guilt inherent in their gross crime of negligence. Hinemoana had been wronged but life must go on, and so must the party. Who were they to destroy the impending pleasure of the myriads of people, including a few friends, who waited all week for their party.

How dare either of them think that just because they felt remorseful and should be kneeling on a wooden floor banging their foreheads at regular intervals with a hard-covered edition of the Bible or the Koran, that they could neglect their individual and collective duties to their guests. After all, it is the modern world and the utilitarian principle must rule, that is how it is on this bitch of a world!

About twenty people had arrived by the time their trauma had ended. Irish whiskey had been designated the drink of the evening and so far there was about three quarters of a bottle average for each drinking guest. Patrick Mika picked up the nearest bottle and pondered the inevitable self- destruction involved if such liquor passed his lips. Having reached some decision he said, 'Enough!' and took a large swig from the bottle.

Paul Te Ariki, sensing his friend's mood, felt a certain twinge of guilt but realising the impossibility of remedial action grabbed the nearest bottle of Tulamore Dew and drank as though it were mothers' milk. Soon they were both on the road to becoming social animals, two introverted worms turning into beautiful, witty butterflies who hand out small portions to people who come to see them for a one-night stand and fall.

It was now about half an hour after pub-closing time and the swell of people into the small house had become overwhelming. Dozens of fragments chipped form the solid block of humanity were scattered, stumbling and moaning, laughing and frantic, about the few rooms in all manner of poses and positions. Each person jostling and hustling, arriving and innocently looking and hoping to find his or her place in the light of the fifty watt light bulb.

Destiny and fate and any number of philosophical viewpoints (lubricated) by alcohol and drugs and many splendid things, were combining to form a new galaxy, a microcosm of universal proportion. A world-view was forming, one which had never previously existed, a unique entity in which each person participated, oblivious to, and yet an integral part of the individual events and ideas, occurrences and utterances: but although asleep to particulars each person was aware of an overall significance, an underlying sense of collective consciousness, which none could understand if called upon to annunciate, but which was, nonetheless, felt with intensity of the strongest passion.

Drunk and melancholy Paul Te Ariki didn't want to spoil the party 'so I'll go' he said to himself and walked the city streets, barely aware of anything apart from an overwhelming sadness and disillusionment with himself and thus the whole of humanity. Even vague contemplation of his relationship with the universe did not humble or console him and as he wandered aimlessly on he began to think of the fog, which was low and thick, as a personification of his limited life and knowledge and his heart sank deeper and deeper, as he thought, 'For I shall suffer, no doubt about that.'

He had walked for nearly ten minutes engrossed in his personal depression when he chanced upon a lamp-post with a street name plate attached. Dundas Street, the name registered in his mind like a dull memory and he muttered exhaustedly to himself. 'So it is Dunedin' he murmured drearily as he walked towards the grim Moloch of the scene and fell silent. The old city, where they build three thousand chimnies and lined them up so it will look like one from a certain point and three thousand from another point, something akin to Coronation Street, like.

Paul Te Ariki crossed the Leith Bridge and began the assent to the brow of the hill which was marked by Clyde Street on his right and Lovelock Avenue on his left. A solitary car passed which he cursed for its intrusion in his painful peace. When he reached the two roads running off Dundas Street he stopped and pondered his immediate future fate. If he went backwards he would be doing what most repelled him after physical contact: that is he would be taking step backwards.

If he went forwards it would mean he would just wander on through the streets of Dunedin with the same purposelessness with which he had pursued the occupation till now, so that going forwards would amount to nothing more than going backwards in the opposite direction there was nothing he resented more than the ironies of nature playing their inexorable tricks on him, although he delighted in their workings on others.

If he went to Clyde Street he could visit a friend but that would be cheating and cowardly-defying the indifference of nature with the warmth of friendship was, to Paul Te Ariki, the ultimate side-step, the farandole, the fling, the brawl, the fandango, the umbowa, the watusi, the twist of the existential dilemma, (a twist of lemming, O'Dorolo) a first-resort and thus a surrender of all principles that were sacred.

His final choice lay in the upward path to the Northern Cemetery: Dunedin is the only city in New Zealand with a stereo system for its dead. It would appear to an astute outsider, say someone from Oamaru, that the living heart of Dunedin, the city, was flanked and amplified by its two main cemeteries, Northern and Southern. Both are situated in places of such significance that few people, except those who live in Dunedin, could fail to recognise the metaphorical significance, like two from another point.

So, like so many aspects of this Scot-Goth city, the dullness of its present generation of citizens is matched only by the ironic brilliance and foresight of past generations. With the aid of chopping logic, Paul Te Ariki turned to the left and ascended slowly into the thickness of the mist and fog of Lovelock Avenue. After five minutes walking he reached the gates of the graveyard and stood transfixed for several moments.

Eventually he entered through the straight, ominous gates. Everything had an ethereal air about it. The tombstones stood almost unseen like rocks in murky water. Paul Te Ariki felt that he was some ancient fish swimming through the ruins of some neglected Atlantis. The further he moved away from the outer perimeter of the cemetery the stronger he felt pulled towards its centre.

He gathered momentum as some unseen force pulled him with magnetic strength through the city of the dead. He no longer was aware of himself but only existed as a movement. He had no control or perception, even though he may be charged with mysticism, Behmenism, quietism, it didn't matter for he was directed by a supernatural agent so that he had become spirit.

In this form he could only feel that he was being moved or maneuvered through objects and over objects which merged and seemed to lose their material life, thus to make a sculpture to put on a mountain for people to see with telescopes. Faster and faster his life-force flowed until he felt like the wind, swift and unseen, blowing and swirling round and round and up and down and everywhere and anywhere. Just when he felt without fear, that he might lose his existence altogether and evaporate into nothingness his curious movements stopped and Paul Te Ariki fell, exhausted and weak, to the ground, *he does not move.*

Paul Te Ariki lay thus for several minutes, almost asleep, until his glance chanced upon a figure, barely discernible in the fog and darkness, standing not twenty feet from him. With a great effort he got himself up off the ground and stood limply against a crumbling headstone. The figure before him did not move and although his senses were returning Paul Te Ariki could not see it any clearer than before, such was the density of the weather and darkness.

As he gained in strength he decided to approach the apparition. Silently he moved forward, his senses alert, his reflexes on the ready. Closer and closer he moved and only slowly did any discernible human features reveal themselves. He saw that the figure was naked and that it was a woman's body. Long hair fell over her breasts and she was standing upright. He tried to speak but words had left him long ago, which was so far to go, so he moved very slowly forward, outside time without extension. As he got within arm's length of the person in front of him he had a sudden realisation and his heart almost leapt out of his mouth.

Paul Te Ariki gave a loud exclamation of bewildered joy and then just as suddenly became as deathly quiet. 'E Hine,' he said in a whisper. The figure did not respond in any way so Paul Te Ariki reiterated, 'Hinemoana' slightly more forcefully this time. Still no reaction, so with much hesitancy Paul Te Ariki moved forward and touched his beautiful, misplaced lover. As his hand moved around her shoulder he had the oddest sensation. He found that this Hinemoana of his was two dimensional. After his first bewildered realisation he examined her closer and sure enough, here was a life-sized cardboard cut-out, complete with backing stand, of his beloved Hinemoana. He wanted to laugh and he wanted to cry, he was violent and helpless, amused and confused ...

At this point Paul Te Ariki woke up from his dream and felt an acute-sense of disorientation as well as the most outrageous hangover headache he had ever experienced. Half-remembering his dream, and half-remembering the nightmares of the party the previous night, he stumbled out of his bed with the idea of making a good strong cup of hot, black coffee. At that moment he heard an agonised groan come from the depths that was Patrick Mika's bed ... use ready-made objects that you can find in your apartment, in other words, Ni gheallfad uaim duit duais nios mo ... no more rewards can be promised so all hehears is the evening train heading towards Puketaraki past 339 and his melancholia is compleat ... quam immolando totius mundi tribuisti relaxam delicta. Per Dominum ... ut per haec piae placationis officia perpetuam misercordiam consequatur Per Dominum nostrum, and suffers like the devine Miranda ... so a woman's secret is different toa man's even unto death, she thought to himself, and she heard the priests last drones ... et in nomine patri, et filu, et spiritus santus aman (amine) and she, Sistermaryhimself shehe would have to confess allher known and unknown sins: past and future in thought, word and deed (indeed), through myfault, throughmy fault, through my most grevious fault ... being aman anda woman there was so many sins and temtations to reveal and reject, so many more evil thoughts and words and deeds to do and think about: how could shedo it and not leave somthingout ... as she made her way from the church to the separate building where there's a guy whosegot religionhe'll tell youif your sin's original, she noticed that the brandnew trolleybus, which replaced Billythebus and Teddy (the toxin) tram had lost its poles off the wire at threelamps ... as she looked out through the eyeofgod shesaw, seesaw, forty yearson ... (13) orthere abouts, people bleeding to death in the morning ara by the sea Hinemoana and the restwerein mourning, ashelooked out from pari Hinemoana as dusk of the secondday of massacre descended the usual beauty of southern evening the evilsoul of people abstracted itself like a hidden andun seen surrealmontage ... centturies oldland scape against minutes old murder, just round the corner, littlejack, historical murderingbeach just round the reverse corner hysterical scenes of death, nonbreath, bereavement sadnessin responseto madness ... another persongone porangi but it wasn't that easy, shit, T.V. image versus tranquil antiquity of the reality of the eyo god ... evil sin evils in the heart of people this time expressed in semi-automatic style, bulletsbang and the coastghost is resurrected, everything looks good in black and white, kodachrome through the third eye, greyimages, dullness of spirit, describedagain Sister, godeeper the eyogod is thefu turetobe, or not tobe the same as the past, present us Sister with the facts ... a house is burnedout ... the deathtoll mayrise, allsouls daymass ... whatever happens the death toll will rise, he wishes she was here withhim, like your master's kingdom our lovecrypt perhaps, cannotbe of this world ... but he loves her just the same, his passion permeates the daysemotion, looking out to the ocean, pacific, unlike the events of the northern headlands, the spit the spirit of ancient pre-verbal com ... no com ... no com ... union (unholy) had the? so surely not but you neverknow do you ... BANG, BANG you're dead, a bullet hereanda bullet there, here abullet, there abullet, everywherea bulletbullet ... but that's not for forty years, she thought do I haveto confess that as theeye of god closes yet again on humanaffairs (all he wants is a humanaffair with her, that's one thing for sure, sharing warmth and love and humour they know is in both of their hearts but the risksare great) evenboats can't enter the harbour as sheenters the confessional shedoes the signof thecross and saysto herself 'I cannot prevent what will happenin AraHinemoana, I cannot Save AraHinemoana from my vision of carnage but 1 will prayfor the living and the dead' ... the trains stillrumble past, and is allaround but their sightis un seen, even the trees that normallyblock knowledge (visual a visual train) cantbe seen because of blackness since the death of Bishop Berkeley, melancholia or otherwives that's the way itgoes, tusalava ... only twentyfour hours from tusalava, onlyone dayaway from id dhoid, or thereabout ... titiro ki te whetu whero, ai whetu whero-whakara i te rau o te patu ... who said that ... there is some thingin theair ... meahiccup meahiccup meahiccuphiccup andeven asshe spoke this visionof terror in futuretimes distressed blessme fatherfor I havesin nedit is twodays today sincemy last con fess ion aeons itseems like light years agoand it seemslike yes terday but notto lotto day and since then I have ... silence descended like the blanket of nightfall on the unsuspectingland butit was uneasy, shit, and her mind was like a wallof graffiti just before itis discovered bya righteous up standing member ... the stillness inside that little box was notcalm but menacing, threatening likea darkalleyway whereyou can still seeshadows and flickers of lightand life, also, the weight should be immense or constantly changing ... kaore mataku au, shethought kia kaha au!, and with this she said, while the priest listened, relieved that sound of windandlimb signifying something had again entered the worldof light ... I have never fucking sinned in my fucking life, shebe gan slowlyand deliber atelymutedelatedly ... notin action (killed inaction means action) no I have never doneone fuckingthing that couldbe interpreted (letsnot pretend) as being bad, but ... at this the priesthe recovered from his reeling shocksand prepared for after shocks which he knew wouldbe morede vastating because now that the found ations have been shaken itwas only left for the edifaces and erections to fall ... nungoeson mangoes in syryp eatall, sickly ... ina jar allways keep a jar of new jam on the windowsill leaving the window ajar har har har ha har ... the sewer of nunsmind is seeping somany some, any years of blocked emotion, effluent pours fluently out through pores of souls and other holes such as assholes, one word she has saidbe forein secret, secretion of shit sap and nuncum ... 1 have had somany sodomy (like a romany my mother said I nevershould) times forlornly forn icated in my mindseye and otherplaces 1 have eaten dogs shit and pulled mybra (not unlike a sticky hydra) and pants down, a clown in front of young children and bade them come and touch me asof I them, touch me badly like an evil forbidden fruit ... Avenged! I turned on and got turned onby, the gas ovens of Triblinka, I didn't even blink as I wat ched all them people dying by myhand you under stand that when I was a child on myfirst holy communion I vowed to Jesus never to sin and in doingso 1 have neverstopped sinning since, for a dream you dream alone may be a dream, but a dream two people dream together is a reality ... know ledge, the ledge of knowing over whichis going my thoughtsof goodand evil, shooting rapids of words and deeds liftup your dress, takedown your tweeds: shakedown, a genuine half-hunter ... fucka duck comecuntcum quid pro quo away wego with a great big negro mutherfucker (yes that too) incest a game the whole family can play gameatazoa tis as gayas theycome ACDC ETC but the worst ofall is I know when to stop ... I have pure shit thoughts pureshit father pureshit but live a life of purityand chast titty who wants a titty tit swill de, tit willdo and a dildo, and a silly vicious bob dyldo at, but why wherefor art the bigcock and the tightlittlecunt of desire how can I goon thinking thus and living thither, help me shithead for I have tinned thyballs and willyeat them for gaters with potaters and shesobbed out of relief and grief, shehad wanted to tell himof her really being a man, not a transvesper exactly to supply scissors for tuc and cuck, old, but a real man except with awo mans body bo-didly bo-didly and there was somuch left unsaid and uncovered ... the priest, whowas really the skull of Samuel Becket inside whicha light shone at regular intervals, an affectation of acting tobe sure or Not I says he and which had being travelling through the suburbs eightfoot tall on the back ofa trailer leaning the righthemisphere and nowlies splitin two Onehunga (there are many hungry, but only One hunger, hey-up, Uncle Fred) keeping the wood from the door, slowly says to her, sister I feel your anguish, I feel your pain

... absolution, and your penance is three hail marys and one how's your father ... come in peace, go in pieces I'll see you round the back in fifteen minutes ... like two colourless orshould I say blackandwhite angels they flewtogether on their wings of desire and landing neara town called Munchen they thought they metall the people they knew, all the people of this Germancity were people they, of course, didntknow but theyall had faces and bodies and clothes of the two angels dearest friends but they didnt know them sothey sattogether in the cafe taking timeout to begin toget to know each other like twopeople whohad just met holding handsand talking forhours andhours then they flewoffsky ward over Poland and sepa rated agreeingto meetin the dream in Los Angeles or New York whence heandshe would dream in Ireland but the heangel was lastseen heading towards the city of the angels (lost) faithless and unfaithful giving in to temporal temptations as the express thundered through the night of the nineteen fourties. I've got to meether, I've got to meether clickety clack clickety clack I've got to meether like a meercat, and clickety clack so the angels were human afterall, should have stayed for lunchin Munchen munch munch, Fred had just brought Alex's afternoon tea, with a chocolate biscuit and his pills. Bruno had been discussing the *egoistisch* concept with Magic Rubezahl and he turned to Fred and said 'Wot abort tha *Id* then Oxo,' ...

At this point an e-mail arrived from Germany advising Alex Munchausen he had won the:
LOTTO: Rheinland-Pfalz
Ferdinand-Sauerbruch-Strasse 2 DE-56073
Koblenz,
Rheinland-Pfalz,
Germany.
Reference Number: LRP/19-DE/9317
Batch: LRP/06/41
CONGRATULATIONS
This E-mail is to inform you that you emerged a winner of 1,000,000 (One million Euro) on our online draws which was conducted last month. Your email address drew the lucky numbers 3-24-1-10-49-17 which consequently emerged you as one of first fifty (50) lucky winners in this category. No tickets were sold. For further Information about your Winnings,contact our Lottery Fiduciary Agent with the following address, stating clearly your reference and batch numbers ...

... butnow the nun Sistermaryhimself was preparing toleave, Adieu! Adieu! even though she hadnt told all, shestill had sinon her soul she still had dreams andmad ness (the locked up monster) she wouldwander to the end of her time with the spectre of darkness in her heart but as sheheard the priest's footfalls coming across to give herher penance she couldnot stand the thought of himbeing on topof and inside her hisgrunting and snorting of sexualstabs madeher feelrepulsive for whileshe knew the virginbirth was an almighty cockup shehad little hope for the Lord's earthly minions, mini ons, soshe ranfor it rather than stay waiting forit, she then exhorted herself not to look at Rock Hudson, but only Doris Day ... when she was young kidsused totalk of digging ahole to China through the earth so S. M. Himself pickedupa spade and with the thought 'I'lldiga hole to Ireland,' she set to work ... when she haddug enough (two miles as the wormflies) a greathunger setin, soshe rested anyway and hermind went straight out of it justas the priest Father O'Blivion had disappeared through the blackhole of hermind asshe had hoped and not through the blackhole of herbody as he hadhoped, nunshe thought howshe blasphemed and that more through crowded confused streets, jumpeda board anold photograph (or wherethey alwaysyou) pera i te marama kahuna kou i another porangi kaere au i mohio ana otira rete he tamaititangohia ia tahi hikoi precious andhid den while studying at Trinity hewas usinghis position as she used violent stabswithher fingers asthe childis afraid of falling this karanga of the poly nesian woman before he drewhis handand made aswipe and letfly, mercy ofgod the sunhad just burstthrough and was in the eyes or he'd beenleft fordead, God hewas nearly sentinto the confetti graveyard about the earlike (better buyan earwig to keep the hearingwarm) a message to the hearingvolk, listen! forall the populace shouting another, a not her round as the laughing forseen poteen event was stopped from having him P.S.M. dragged along like anold tinbox chattering along the street, kept mefromgo inginsane, life wenton like that again through a field onher (offer) way the grasswas wet and over leaned the path she heldher skirts sensationally up andnot because thegrass waswet and sweet and sweat o'the brow because aman, P.S.M. was watching she wasin love with passion and its weakness that wetgrass couldnot cool radiated from her unwanted womb in that country, show all the virgins twotogether omnibus style in that metaphysical land (twomiles down) where fieshwas a thought more spiritual (unlike carnal victual) than music. Among the stars out of reachof the peasant hand ... kei te mokemoke au under mountains you carry the weight of my passions she said if you want to callme ina hurry dial nein, nein, nein, in otherwords dont callme! That's the idea, let's make a little conversation - Ich bin von Munchen munch munch, Munchausen Magic Moments is deacair teacht yes I knowbut, about it he is impotent ni feidir leis teacht, d'iarras air teacht: perhaps someone will teach him. Butaft era few daze of diggin it S.M. Him selfish asit was (not shellfish) decided she didnt digit nomore, sowith only as light error of Judgement Day she turned around having goneonly twentyfive (25) miles towards Ireland through the centre of the earth and she came out of the ground near Punakaiki, butthen looked enough for life tobe the Giant's causeway of Ant cluchaun na Vomore ach anyway so giant pancakes it is all round and there's Rita taking her first steps, practicing for alps, out of loneliness and homesickedness, start somewhere you know, youknow. Rita points the bone towards the place of Sister Joyce orat least Joyce's sister who when they meet throws upher armies in exasperation 'an leabhar san Sheamais' and then again, 'an obair seo na Gaelige' but then doesn't she give the nunsister Maryhimself a big welcome to the Westcoast and listens to her story laughing and after the feast of the Iclassl kyrie fans bonitatis kyrie eleison (before kiritekanawa, daughter of ...) gloria in excelsis Deo, daughterof ... Et in terra pax he - minibus to Hokitika, usedtobea railcar from Ross bonae vo-lunta tis laudamus te. Bene Hill dickimus te, you were afraid of the whip. Adoramus te. Glorificamus te, now finish up your tea and we will goto bed ... Sisterjoice and sisterhimself layin eachother's arms afterorgasm both feeling replete, the great togetherness of two people cometogether in love, drifting off to sleep together and separately, whispering the odd involuntary word one to the other meaningless in context but full of the wonder of nomeaning love and ancient knowledge that no wakingday world can understand as their breasts touch each others lightlynow, Gratias agimus tibi propter magnana glorian tuam. Cum Sancto Spiritu in gloria Dei Patris, A-men, you never know when you die, big or small ...

Patrick Mika's Dream
The only time that Fitz did sleep that night he dreamed of her. The dream was so vivid and real and alive that he felt it was more real than things were when he was awake. Together they walked, Te Riro i He and Patrick Mika, through the twilight city. Everything seemed exact and yet dislocated. The old Stock Exchange building was still standing and the pre-neon illuminated clock flashed an iridescent flicker of colour onto the tramlines, extraordinary the tricks that memory plays! It had been raining and the streets looked washed and clean as only summer rain can do. The time flashed again – Kuata pahi ono karaka – followed by the date – Te tekau ma ono o nga ra o Hune; ko te kau kotahi mano iwa rau ma wha – It was their first walk together and they clung to each other like rejoycing barnacles. As the 6.15 tram to Caversham went clanking past they saw a notice that the mayor had asked that the Order in Council for the Andersons Bay tramway might be hurried on.
They walked further away from their timeout to be together place, still locked arm in arm. She was explaining to him how some young women suffered a kind of dying by inches. 'That is the only way to describe hundreds of bloodless girls who are slipping slowly but surely from simple anaemia into a decline,' she was saying. They walked past the bank towards the Octagon. Looking in the window of J & J Arthurs they saw some all-wool Colonial Tweed Suitings for only £2/15s/0d. 'That's cheap,' Hinengaro said, and as they moved further along George Street they discussed the idea of going for a Coach ride to Highcliff and Sandymount. 'Lets go next Tuesday – it's only 1s/6d each way,' Hine said to Mika and everything went red like a lightning flash with colour. Hinengaro Te Riro i He and Patrick Mika were both in love and they walked as if on air. Indeed, the local newspaper said as much as they swung back towards the Octagon, 'truly much is in the air,' to sit silent at the foot of the Poet's statue.
'Doomsblay maybe amidst the smoke of battle, but there is no battle in the smoke of Juno, and Wai Rongoa now holds ten special gold medals,' said Fitz as they walked quickly past Dallas and Watts. It was getting dark now and the last tram up the valley would soon be leaving. What with the death of a footballer and Bibles in schools Fitz could feel the city re-enter his mind and he wished she had been with him. He carried her through the hard-nosed day of a labouring man and her beauty was so strong that he wept inward, 'for no matter how close we get to each other, there is always air between us' ...
Fitz woke up with the image of her in a long flowing early century dress and hat walking down the Boulevard de Dunedineaux, holding his arm as they went window shopping. The absurdity of such a vision made him want to burst out in laughter. The shadows and light of the living room gave a certain surreal aspect when married with his dreams. He fell asleep again and his waka entered into the strange seas of another moemoeä o aroha. This time she came to him brown, bare-breasted, laughing and radiant they felt each other's presence as earth-bound, yet beyond the confines of obstacles – as unchained manacles

released from chains, the uncertain yet true manu o aroha hou was about to express its new freedom Fitz woke up to the sound of the phone ringing ...

Hinengaro's Dream

Lying in the darkened bedroom as the first light of dawn began to rise slowly above the darkness, Hinengaro Te Riro i He realised the enormity and the necessity of what had happened, you don't know whether you're happy or not. Drifting between dreams and sleep, she found herself wandering alone along a desolate beach. Fitz stood solitary at a river mouth and she could see he was wearing a military uniform of some description. She went up to talk to him, touching him softly on the arm. She then saw he was holding a child who had been badly wounded by a bullet. The horizon had an unnatural, ethereal glow - like a sunset in reverse.

Hine took the silent, bleeding child from Fitz and he jumped aboard a tank which was headed towards the front. She was overcome by the stillness, so she dance in pitch dark. He saluted her in a half reverential, half mocking manner and as Fitz and his comrades turned into a cloud of dust she was shocked to see he was wearing an Iron Cross and Oak Leaves with a swastika held in the talons of an eagle. The scene then changed to Te tekau ma ono o nga ra o Hune, ko te tau kotahi. Mano, iwa rau ma wha, and as the tram to Mäori Hill clanked along George Street they looked at each other and burst out laughing. 'We missed our tram again, eh Miki!' she said. 'Oh well, we wouldn't want to be the only Maoris living in Mäori Hill!'

'Anyway, is the game worth the candle?' Fitz mused enigmatically as they walked further back arm in arm towards the Octagon, where they sat silent at the foot of the Poet's statue. This was the first day they had walked out together and both were wearing their nicest winter DRESS MATERIALS, which they had purchased from THE DUNEDINERS, Dallas and Watts (The Dead). Hine had remembered seeing the ghost of J.S. Grant, who only two years before had been on these streets hawking his sad little masterpiece of woeful thinking, *A Tale of Horror*.

Hine laughed as she recalled to Miki how she had just made the late letters guard's van of the Port Train at 2.30 that afternoon. 'I told him in the epistle in no doubtful language the result after taking Dr. Morse's Indian Root Pills and that tomorrow everything will be better,' she said almost in hysterics. Having a discrete shot of Wolfe's Schnapps (for kidney ailments, naturally) they walked, arms linked, along the streets of Dunedin.

Hine felt happy and light, and as they planned a trip by horse and coach together the following Tuesday to Sandymount, she almost forgot her husband and child and the family obligations which stood between them like trees against the horizon. The best thing was that they were happy, in future times they might have a dance party. Suddenly the dream darkened, as though the Sow of Hades had descended, her dark shadow throwing everything into evil contrast and premonition of the winds of a terrible century ahead looming.

She had reached te wahi moemoeä and felt afraid as the winds blew hard out along the coast telling of the thousand miles and the millions of murders – a face floated before her from the steam cloud of a locomotive's boiler. She followed it and saw its Moko engraved on its surface. The Moko told an ancient story of Abelard and his niece and their ill-fated love. He ended up a ball-less theologian and she a nun ... Kei te kata nei ano, kua mane te ngakau, a, te mutunga o taua koa he pouri ... the cloud face, smiling down at her, was that of Mika leading her closer and closer towards the cliffs which overlook the sea at Parimoana.

Then she was falling – falling down all the years from 1904, down the thousand miles from Tamaki ma kaurau to Otepoti, the day she threw herself into the Rhône, through the murderous fog which was the Sow of Hades, over the wild cliffs of Parimoana, falling, falling and he keeps calling me back again ... 'Wake up, Hine! Wake up!' It was her Blooming husband, Paul, calling her. 'You must have been having a nightmare – it's alright, darling,' he said, and she held him close and he stroked her hair soothingly, *they do not move.*

But hemika went on dreaming until he became Alex the Magic Munchausen whose friend Bruno was at that moment telling a 'Goodnight' (now the Sun turns out his light) story to him, even though it was only just after tea-time, (same as yesterday, ham and eggs – and just these few pills like a good boy) which began 'in the town where I was born' ... but went on to become the Mäori version of Kaipuke Ruku Wai Köwhai iti, in other words Alex, in his Te Ariki manifestation, was returning to one of his childhoods, traveling through light, time and sound in a fantastic voyage which he hoped would not turn to erosion in his shrunken head yellow submarine manned by Munchausen Moments of memory and fantasia in the guise of two tigers ... Rakai and Rewa are leaving their homeland for Aotearoa ...

'Ssshhh, come and look at Rakai and Rewa, Molly Monkey.'

'I saw them before Gigantic Giraffe, they were going for a walk.'

'What are you doing hitching a ride again on my head Frederick the great Frigate Bird!'

'I wanted to see Rakai the Great and Rewa the Beautiful, the tigers who moved further into the jungle to escape from the hunters of the Hercinian forest.'

'Ssshhh,' said Molly again, 'listen to what they're saying.'

'We'll have to move again tonight, Rakai.'

'You're right' growled Rakai 'those hunting drums are getting closer.' Giant Giraffe whispered, 'Look at those flashing large, sharp teeth.'

'They must be the biggest and fiercest in the whole world.'

'Ssshhh, or he might use them on you, then you'll not only be the silliest monkey in the jungle, but we'll have to change your name to Minced Monkey eh Fred, hee, hee, hee!'

'I'm annoyed at always having to shift places to escape the people who want to kill us, Rewa.'

'I know, so am I. We've had a kai, now let's go to sleep so that we will be strong for our journey tonight.'

'Good idea, ggrrrrowwwll, good night Rewa.'

'We'll keep a watch in turns, O.K. Frederick and Molly. I'll go first, because I can see the hunters coming from miles away with my long neck.' 'They're coming, they're coming, warn Rakai and Rewa!!!' Sneaky Snake suddenly shouted to the animals.

'Wha, wha, what's happening?'

'You silly monkey! You were meant to be on look-out, not sleeping. The hunters have arrived to capture Rakai and Rewa! Can't you hear their guns and shouts?' BANG! BANG! BANG! BANG! 'There they are, let's get them!'

'Quick, this way Rakai, Rewa, there's no time to lose. The hunters are almost here! Follow me along this secret path, Fred and I will take you both to the witch-doctor who will help you escape.'

The frigate bird flew ahead, coming back every now and then to report to the giraffe.

'One more river to cross, chirp, chirp, only one more river to cross and we'll be there.'

BOOM! BOOM! BOOM! BOOM! 'The drums are following us, hurry, hurry! Come on Rakai and Rewa, you can make it!'

'We're trying our best, giraffe, but we are still half asleep.' The two tigers said, struggling to keep up with their tall friend.'

'You'll be dead if you don't stop talking and start running. Boy, I never thought I'd be talking like this to a tiger!!!' Giant Giraffe whispered.

'There it is, there's the clearing - run Rakai, run Rewa, run to the witch-doctor's protection area!'

BOOM! BOOM! BANG! BANG! The terrifying sound of guns of Hul and Chul and Uz and their drums and guns and guns and drums, hoorah, hoorah, grew nearer as the the village witchdoctor appeared.

'Rakai and Rewa' he said, 'I have a spell which will save your lives -
the chant I say you must repeat'

we are the tigers, the hunted ones
they come to kill us with their guns

for love of greed and lust for power
the evil hunters try to possess
the beauty of the coat of Rewa
and from Rakai his prowess

but this spell will enshroud
us in the safety of a long, white cloud
which will protect us from all ill and harm
but in accepting this magic charm
we place ouselves in a state of exile
from sight and sound, away many a mile

'This means,' said the witch-doctor, 'you will only exist in dreams and visions in the far off land of Aotearoa.'

'We can't do anything but accept, Rakai.'

'I know,' he said, and they kissed for the last time in the physical world.

'Quick, the hunters are here, the bullets are hot around our heads!'

'Where did they go!'

'They were here, they just disappeared.'

'Rubbish! Two tigers can't just vanish. O.K. old man, where did the tigers go?' The witch-doctor looked at the head hunter without saying a word.

'But boss, it's true - they just disappeared into thin air - we burst into the clearing, I had them dead in the sights of my rifle, and whoosh they went into nowhere. I was so suprised I dropped my *ger* and nearly fell over backwards!'

The boss was really angry,

'What do you know about all this mumbo-jumbo?' he turned on the old man who he was sure knew what had happened. But before he could strike him a cry of horror pierced the jungle air.

'Aaaaeeeee!!!!! Look! The sky!'

'Oh no!'

'It's turned the colours of the tigers' coats. It's a curse!'

'We're all doomed. Run, run - I'm a gettin' outa here!!!'

'Come back you cowards, come back! Don't be so superstitious - we've still got to hunt down the ferocious three-toed-sloth!'

The evil boss was left standing alone looking at the setting sun which had streaks of orange, yellow and black light flashing across the horizon like an enormous vision of Rakai and Rewa. 'It's just like a magic carpet' cried Rewa excitedly as they flew high above the clouds in their wakamoehewa.

'Wheeeeeeeee' the tigers yelled as they rode the currents and waves of the air like *freigelassenen*.

'It's like a waka riding the ocean waves, hold on tight Rewa,' Rakai called.

'The sky's so dark, it's the deep purple of night and our waka wheels and reels through the bilowing clouds like a space ship.'

'We must be the first ever flying tigers,' Rakai yawned, 'I tired. Let's go to sleep, we've had a big day. I'll set a steady course for the waka.'

'Look Rakai,' whispered Rewa. 'Look, the southern sky is showing the first thin slither of light and there's the rim of the long, white cloud in the distance. It is real, our new home is real.'

Tipi tipi rere rä i te Hinemoana, kia tau ki Te Ika a Mäui.

WAIATA
When Rakai the Great
and Rewa the beautiful
were threatened by death
and destruction

they believed in the power
of dreams and magic
to save their lives which
helped them find a solution

The tigers explore their new home with their friends, Rangi and Hine. *Kei rö moenga e moemoeä ana ngä tokorua nei.*

'Rakai! Rakai! Wake up! Wake up! Look at the beautiful red flowers. *E oho! E oho! Titiro ki ngä hua räkau nei, he putiputi tino ätaahua.*'

'Uh, uh, aahhhh!!' the big tiger stretched, 'what did you wake me up for to show me some stupid flowers. You know what I'm like in the morning, gggrrroowwlll.'

'But look, Rakai, our waka came to rest on a beach and the whole beach front is ablaze with the red flowers,' she said excitedly.

'Here's one to wear behind your ear, Rewa. I'm sorry, I was just tired and still dreaming.'

'They are Pohutakawa,' a voice said.

'Who's there, who's that?' the tigers became alarmed.

'I thought the witch-doctor said nobody could see us, Rakai I'm afraid.'

Ko mäua ngä tïpuna o te iwi Mäori

'Kia ora, ngä tipuna Taika my name is Rangi. Only me and the other children can see you, so don't be scared, I'm not *Irmin the German* or anyone: the adults with the guns won't know you're here.'

'We've been looking for you everywhere. I'm Hine, Rangi's sister and we recognized you as our ancestors because of your moko.'

'What a lovely welcome to our new home, Rakai.'

'What's a moko, Hine? Oh, by the way, my name is Rakai and this is Rewa.'

'The moko are the facial markings which tell the story of the person wearing them and they look very like the designs on your faces, eh Rangi.' 'Let's light a fire on the beach,' said Hine.

'Yeah! Then we can have a kai and a korero with our new ancestors!' replied Rangi. They all sat round a fire and the tigers told the children of the adventures on their journey to Aotearoa.

'And then we saw the long white cloud in the distance and when we woke up you were standing there looking at us, Rangi.'

'And then I came along, eh!' said Hine and they all laughed.

'Why don't we go exploring, we'd really like you and Rangi to show us around our new home of Aotearoa, wouldn't we Rakai!' The big tiger growled in approval.

'Me and Rangi have got special secret powers, just like you and Rewa. We can see people and things from the past that other people can't see.'

'And we can introduce you to the people from legends, even the Frisii, Fasi, Dulgibines, Ambrones, Tubantes:' Rangi added excitedly, 'you know, the ones that other people say don't exist anymore.'

Pënei tonu i a mäua nei, i takahia e mäua te huarahi i parahia e o mäua mätua tïpuna, arä rä, e o tätau mätau tïpuna.

'Leave the wakamoehewa on the beach. We'll go into town on the Pahi, you two won't even have to pay because the driver won't be able to see you, neat eh!'

'Look Rakai, Look! Instead of the animals in this jungle having feet and legs and paws all the creatures here have got round things underneath them and they all roll along on them instead of walking!'

'And see that Rewa,' laughing at the top of his terrible tiger voice, 'all those animals have people inside them. Look, you can see them through their transportation transparent skins. Ha, Ha, Ha, they must have eaten them for dinner last night!' The two tigers were relishing the sight of the humans inside these animals.

'They can go pretty fast, those huanimals.'

'Just like our old friend, Jeff Jaguar, back home, eh Rakai! Hey! What are you two giggling at? Come on, out with it Hine.'

'Yeah, what's so funny Rangi?' asked Rakai.

'It's just ... ha ha ha ... it's just that ... HA HA HA - Oh, I can't say it without bursting out laughing - You tell them, Hine ... ha ha ha!'

'Well, those things you thought were called animals are actually cars. Ha ha ha. And people made them so they can go faster than they normally do. But the funny thing was when you were talking about your friend, Jeff, a car went by which is called a Jaguar. Ha! Ha! Ha!'

'We'll get this bus,' said Rangi.

'So this is one of the bigger wheeled animals called ABUS, otherwise known as Almenden' Rewa asked.

'The animals and people in this jungle are quite different from home, eh Rewa.' Rakai looked out from the window as the big yellow bendy banana bus headed into the city.

'They build their houses high into the sky, not like the people back home whose dwellings are low to the ground and sometimes even in the ground.'

'It's quite scary, eh Rakai. Even though no-one can see us and nothing can touch us, all the noise and the constant activity of the people and their wheeled animals never seem to rest, they move continuously it seems, just for the sake of it, even in the heat of the middle of the day.'

Kei te hurihuri haere i te ao o whätonga.

'Who are those really big birds called Wakarererere that fly over the city making a deafening sound and those big long animals with many legwheels which looked like the largest snakes they had ever seen, Hine?'

Titiro, te nunui o ënei neke.

'Don't be frightened, you two. They're called planes and trains. People travel around inside them the same as a bus. Maybe we've had enough for one day, let's get the next bus back. Anyway, you're wakamoehewa will be wondering where you are.'

E whakaae ana mäua he pahi te neke, he neke te pahi.

'E, kui,' Hine asked her old auntie that night, 'can there be tigers in New Zealand?' Auntie Mere thought for a while and said,

'No! ... but if you believe it then there is! You kids should sneak in and uncover the mirror that your mum covers over at night and if you see tigers there, then they exist!'

'Thanks Auntie,' she said.

'Hey Rangi, you kow how mum always covers up any mirrors in the whare at night and shuts all the drawers and cupboards ... to keep the ghosts out.'

'Or maybe to keep them from coming out, because that's where they live all the time!' said Rangi and both the children said at once, and giggled he he he.

'Good night, Rewa and Rakai, our new ancestors!' And they went to sleep dreaming of the trip they were going on tomorrow with their tiger friends like the expedition of Brennus to Delphi.

WAIATA
The road lies before us
Fearful and fearsome
Is our stance
As we prepare to leave

Kähore anö au kia kite i te neke pënä rawa te roa.
Kei te kite këhua kë koe. Kähore hoki räua i konei.

Gone will be our protection
Of friends and whanau
We will stand alone
Against the wind and snow

Kähore anö au kia kite i te neke pënä rawa te roa.
Kei te kite këhua kë koe. Kähore hoki räua i konei.

The Wakaneke Kehua to Rotorua

'This train-animal reminds us of one of our friend back home, eh Rakai.'

'Old Jaunty Python, he was a friendly and jolly fellow for a snake - instead of running away all the village children would run to greet him as he emerged from the jungle.'

'And Jaunty would take ten or more of them at a time for a ride on his back, so big and powerful was his body, a bit like this new train-snake,' Rewa added, laughing.

'I bet those who ended up going for a ride inside him weren't very amused, unlike this wakaneke.'

'That's true, Rangi,' Rewa replied thoughtfully.

Just then the train let out a great roar. Wooooowoooo!!!!!

'What was that?' Rakai asked in a frightened voice.

'Don't worry,' Hine replied, 'its not a lupomaniac, it's only the train blowing its whistle.'

'Where we came from snakes are always very quiet and move softly so no one could hear them coming.' Rewa said, slightly confused.

'Things are certainly different in Aotearoa,' Rakai said, 'even the reason for our journey is very strange. Why are two tigers going on a tiger hunt?'

'The train has just left Morrinsville Station,' Hine interrupted Rakai. 'Before we do any 'tiger hunting' we have to go and visit some people who lived long ago.'

'And between here and there we will see some old kehua Railway Stations that most people think don't exist anymore,' Rangi added excitedly.

'They are the ones with the Mäori names only. Adults without the magic vision can't see them, just like they can't see tigers. But the four of us know that the past and the ancestors are still very much alive.'

'SSSOOOOOOOODDDDOOOOOO I, WWWOOOOO!!!!!!!'

'Wow! Did you hear that? The train knows what we do too! How awesome,' Hine added in surprise, while the Jomsvikinger Band played ...

'Clickety clack, Karikiti karakiti - KIWITAHI

The single kiwi struggles with his mahi' the wakaneke said as they passed the first Mäori Railway Station.

'We're well on the way now, we're on the Waikato - Rotorua line!' Hine was almost leaping from her seat.

'Clickety clack, Kaikiti karakiti - WAHAROA

The great mouth opens for you, e hoa'

'How amazing!' said Rewa, 'this train must have been a Te Reo poet all these years, and nobody ever knew.'

'That's pretty weird. When we just stopped at Matamata to pick up those passengers the train-poet didn't say anything.' Rangi was thinking deeply aloud and did't hear the guard call out,

'All tickets please!'

'Clickety clack, Karikiti karakiti - HINUERA

Hot, burning oil, ai, really hinu-wera'

'What did you say?' the guard said to Rangi suspiciously. 'I know you cheeky Mäori kids, you think you can get away with murder, swearing in your language and then acting dumb. Anyway, you'll have to give up your seats at Putaruru because there's lots of adults getting on.'

'But what about our friends,' Hine burst out before she realized what she had said.

'Clicketyclack Karikiti karakiti - OKOROIRE
I ate the white necked-duck said the old kiore'

'That was close' said Rangi in a hushed voice. 'If the train hadn't been talking about the rat or the dingbat or the Dingstatt or the Thing that ... the guard would have heard you yelling about Rakai and Rewa.'

'Don't worry about it little brother. He would have thought I was porangi anyway.'

'Wouldn't be far wrong would he?'

'Aaauuueee!!!' Hine replied, giving her brother a good clip on the ear.

Clickety clack, Kaikiti karakati – TIRAU

Ko te wakaneke e rere ana, ko te kāuka e rere ana, ko te upoko e nuku ana. Tau ana te rangimārie. He tinihanga pai noa iho.

From train's window the cabbage-trees number rau.

'It's funny how every time we go past a ghost-station with a Māori name the train always makes a little poem,' said Rewa.

'The poet-train is just like us, Rewa. Only Rangi and Hine can hear him, the same as they are the only ones who can see us.'

'And ...'

'Ladies and gentlemen, we are about to enter the station at Putaruru.' The guard announced over the intercom.

'... how the train-poet goes quiet when we get to a station where people get on and off.' Rakai was continuing when the guard came and said to Hine and Rangi, 'Come on you rascals, stand up for the adults, and tell your invisible freinds to get up too. We don't normally allow tigers on these trains so count yourselves lucky I don't put you all off at Putaruru. Come on,' he said laughing, 'come on, we haven't got all day!'

The children giggled as theystood up and moved to the back of the carriage. Rakai said confusedly, 'How come the guard knows about us, and how come he gives you both a hard time when he's a Māori himself?'

'E, ngā tipuna tika, now you're beginning to learn about us and yourselves, eh! After all those years of living in the serious jungle where life was simple and all you had to do was find someone to eat, you come here and find your ancestors and mokopuna are all a bunch of tricksters. Also, the Reiks were always priests belonging to an ancient race. Now you know why you wear a moko too!'

'Clickety clack, Karikiti karakati - NGATIRA
Haere ra, to the parties of travellers, haere ra.'

The poet-snake train began picking up speed as it headed towards the highest point of the railway, the train and all the passengers began to sing the waiata of the railway ...

WAIATA - a chant
'Clickety clack, Karakiti karakati - ARAHIWI
The track to the top past the railway's mahi
Ko ngā pukepuke whenua e kitea nei
Clickety clack, Karakiti karakati - MAMAKU
Don't confuse with Kaponga where there is Mamaku

Ko te rito o te Mamaku ko te oranga tinana
Clickety clack, Karakiti karakati - TARUKONGA
Many lie dead here, before their final *haerenga*
Ko te otaota ko te pukepuke oranga tinana
Clickety clack, Karakiti karakati - NGONGOTAHA
Drink from the mountain fountain calabash, kia kaha!
Ko te tahä inuhia nei ko te oranga tonutanga
Clickety clack, Karakiti karakati - KOUTU
Rotorua projectionist above, no more utu
Ko ngä tohu äta tau, a tata. Ko Rotorua rä tënä
Clickety clack, Karakiti karakati - ROTORUA
Two lakes, passengers, ghosts, tigers in the rain, ua! ua! ua!
Ko ngä roto, ko ngä pähihi, ko ngä këhua. Ka ua, ka ua, ka ua

The children and the tigers met some legendary ancestors of the Rotorua area,
even in places where there was *ne mesa*.
'Look! Look!' cried Rewa, 'Our canoe, our waka has flown here to meet us at the
lake of Rotorua.'
*Äe. E kore rätau e whakapono he waka heke mai i te rangi. Ko te manu anake tä
rätau e möhio nei.*
'And our waka has two of his friends with him, two other canoes to keep him
company' replied Rakai.
'Kia ora!' the waka greeted it's charges. 'Kia ora koutou, I thought I'd better fly
here and meet you all on the lake when you arrived. These are two of my waka
friends I met on the way. This is Matarewhawha the floating log, and this is
Wakawairua, the famous phantom canoe of Tarawera.'
'Kia ora koutou, e hoa ma,' the two canoe-strangers said in unision.
'How great to see our friend who brought us all the way to Aotearoa, come on
Rangi and Hine, lets go down to the lakeside and welcome our friend,' Rakai
said.
But the children went running ... AAAAAAAUUUUUUEEEEEEE !!!!!!! they
screamed, fleeing and hiding behind a bush.
*Auë! Koia nä ngä waka kei runga o maunga Tarawera i kitea e ngä tïpuna i mua
mai i te wä i pahü. He waka këhua kë.*
'What's wrong with you two. Anyone would think you'd seen a ghost,' said Rewa
as the two tigers went after them to see what had frightened their friends. 'We
have! We have!' Rangi and Hine replied together. 'It's ... it's ...'
'Well, this is funny behaviour from the two brave ones who can talk without fear
to two comlpete tiger-strangers!' Rakai said to his two trembling young friends.
'But ... But ... But that's the kehua canoe - the one which people, both Mäori and
Pakeha, saw just before the Tarawera eruption,' stammered Hine.
'Yeah, and the whole area exploded, BANG!!! And all the people got killed,'
explained Rangi.
Suddenly, Wakawairua spoke. 'Don't be afraid children. You are right, it was me
who tried to warn the people of their doom. But they had been greedy and broke
the ancient laws and the earth was angry. But nowadays Matarewhawha and I
are just a couple of old fellas who float around talking about the old days and
enjoying meeting people like you and your tiger friends.'

Matarewhawha now spoke. 'We like to see visitors because not many of those who come to this area, and there are many each year I can tell you, not many of them take the time to come and visit us old kehua. Oh, they are always talking about things we did in the past, but they don't realize we still exist. Mind you, the wahines still won't let us near the *Gadem* or the *Schrein*.'

'Climb aboard,' Wakawairua said. 'Rangi you come with me and Hine can go with Matarewhawha, and Rakai and Rewa can go with their own wakahoa who has carried them so far in the past on their journey to Aotearoa.'

'Where are we going?' the children both asked excitedly at the same time.

'We'll take you all to meet some other ancestors,' the waka replied.

'Yes, they'll be pleased to meet some new children.'

'Also, I doubt whether they've met any tiger-ancestors before. Should be quite a surprise for them, eh Mata, Heh, Heh, Heh.' As the canoes chuckled away to themselves the children and the tigers clambered on to their boats.

'Takes a bit of getting used to,' Mata said to Hine as she struggled to keep her balance.

'Same for you, Rangi. Just put one foot in at a time, hold on to the sides and then lower yourself down slowly,' Waka instructed Rangi kindly. 'Whoooooppss! Nearly went into the drink then, Hine. Just take it easy, that's better. Now sit down on the slats across my middle,' said Mata as the girl worked her way awkwardly into her seat.

Ko eke ngä tamariki ki runga i ngä waka.

'Okay everyone, we're off to Mokoia Island. Follow Mata and me and we'll all get their safely.'

'The lake is beautiful and calm today,' Rewa said to Rakai as their waka friend steered them safely towards the island.

'Who do you think we will meet when we get there?' asked the big male tiger. Before Rewa could answer Matarewhawha pulled up alongside their waka and said,

'We are going to see our old friend Hatupatu. He's getting quite old now, but he can still play a good trick or two like he did on his brothers in the old days. He's still playful but he's not *Versessen* by any taniwha!'

'Ai, he's still a bit of a character. And he still goes walking every day with his friend from the old times, Tamumu-ki-te-rangi. The elderly blowfly flies beside him, telling him bits of news and gossip from his tipi-haere journeys.'

Mata suddenly became excited. 'Look! Look!' he cried. 'Look, there's Hinemoa and Tutanekai. See how graceful and elegant they still are, even after so many years.'

'That's because their love keeps them young,' replied Waka, and they all looked on in wonder.

'That's what Rakai and Rewa will be like in a hundred years,' Hine said and the two tigers blushed. The three canoes pulled up on Mokoia Island's foreshore.

'You people and tigers from the spirit world will be welcome here,' Matarewhawha said quietly, 'for Mokoia is home for the dead as well as the living.'

'The tapu here protects even the smallest beings.' Waka continued and told them more, ending by saying how the little gulls even get protection if they visit.

Ko wai ëra?

Ka ü ngä waka e toru nei ki Mokoia.

'The spirits become part of them also, because their flock leaders are said to be ancient chiefs of the local people. They have *mundium* or guardianship and are the kaitiaki of here.'

'Look, that stone over there, that's a kumara-god' Mata was saying when all of a sudden the mauri of the stone began to chant a waiata, and even though neither Rakai and Rewa nor Hine and Rangi had ever heard the song before Te Matua-tonga filled their hearts with joy and their mouths with song-words and they all sang ...

WAIATA
Who will feast upon and where
The stores of dried fish over there?
The mouths of Mokoia will
Where over-flowing ovens still
Mean a relish of taste for us
Aha! How sweet the potato will be
To go down with the kumara ...
Ai, to go down with the kumara, aue
Down the Backbone and out the Mouth of a Fish
Te ainga tahi te kainga tahi, Hü ... Hü ... Huhua te uri

'I liked the marae best,' Rewa said excitedly, 'especially when they did the wero, that was quite frightening but also really neat.'

'And all the dancing and singing was beautiful - I was sad to leave Mokoia and all our new friends both real and legendary,' Rakai added.

Ko ngä mahi whakangahau, he tino mahi ërä. Te kapa haka. Ngä mahi waiata. Ngä mahi whakataetae. Kore rawa au e wareware.

'Well, maybe we can go back there after we've been to Te Waiponamu, but now we must continue our journey. Come on, all aboard the Wakaneke o Taumarunui,' Rangi cried.

'Are we really travelling down the back of a fish?' Rakai had difficulty understanding the fact that their train was going along the back of Te Ika a Maui.

Hine laughed. 'Yes, we are going down the back of a fish inside a snake, wait when we tell mum and dad that when we get home, eh Rangi - he, he, he, pretty porangi, eh.'

'I only hope that taniwha at Tangiwai doesn't get us,' Rangi said in a funny, almost strange voice.

'Why, what could be worse than that encounter we had with King Ngarara at Waitomo, the place of *Schutz und Schirm, Stein und Bein*, on the way to the station?' asked Rewa.

'Yeah, with all those shining worm light-bulbs and that echo, echo, echo chamber he lived in - it was all pretty weird' Rakai added.

Titiro ki ngä rama iti e tïramarama mai rä.

'Oh, you get used to people-lizards like him. He's quite harmless really, and with his magical third eye he was able to see you two when no-one else could. You're just jealous that he took a liking to Rewa. Anyway, it was nice that he gave us a ride to the station at Taumarunui or we would have had to wait for the night train.'

'Another twelve hours, and in the cold of middle fish - bbbrrrrrrr!' Hine shivered.

'So what's so bad about this Tangiwai taniwha, then?' asked Rakai, still smarting from Rangi's dig about Ngarara's attention to Rewa, but he was interrupted by an excited cry from Hine ... 'Look! Look Rangi, we're going around the famous spiral tattooed on the fishes back. Remember, dad told us about it, about how it was done from the dye of a hundred red-pine rimu trees.'

'Yes,' Rangi replied, 'that's why its called the Raurimu Spiral.'

Taihoa. Kia mau tö koutou pupuri i ö koutou türu.

The wakaneke sped through the landscape south of Rangataua.

Ko Rangataua terä, te käinga o tetahi tino pakanga. I hui ai ngä ope tauä o ngä tïpuna ki reira tohe ai.

'That's where the war parties used to parade in ranks before battle,' Rangi told the two tigers who were looking through the window skin at many strange things which were different to their homeland. At one point whilst observing the beautiful far-off mountains of the centre of the centre of Te Ika a Maui (the fact that the snake was travelling across the back of a fish was very weird to the tigers) they saw a long and winding river leading to the door of the train.

Rangi suddenly called out 'Beware of the taniwha which lives in the Tangiwai river of Aotearoa for it can suddenly swell up and kill a wakaneke just like swatting a fly!!!' The Gepidæ preferred total destruction as the boy went on almost in a frenzy ... 'The taniwha of Tangiwai which did just that has haunted train travellers in this part of the country ever since.'

Äe. He piriti whakawhiti i te awa o Whangaehu i te takiwä o Tangiwai.

When the train had passed over the Tangiwai rail bridge safely Rewa said, 'This reminds me of the Acquatic Anaconda back home who causes havoc amongst the river boat travellers. But among the Catti every boy wore an iron ring on his arm.'

He neke kë rä tënei.

Rakai then added, 'He's a large legendary snake who rose up out of nowhere swallowing boats and barges in one gulp and disappearing back into the depths of dark waters as mysteriously as he had risen from the water - just like your taniwha does to a train!'

The tiger they were hunting sounded very strange indeed. It lived in the far south of Te Waipounamu and was a Scottish tiger which travelled around on wheels through the streets of Otepoti with people inside just like abus or a snaketrain or a carcat. Something else was funny about Aotearoa. Every place seemed to have two names, one in English and one in Mäori and these were the ones which Zubu and Sambo knew more of because they were the ones which Rangi and Hine had taught them in their waka under the pohutukawa trees.

I mahue i te käinga.

Ko tënei kë. Kia hoki mai ä-konahi nei ö tätau mätua tïpuna.

Zubu and Sambo go tiger hunting

a parallel universe to cross (all de children sing)

(lingsong, lingsong, lingsong, tiddle I-po, tiddle eye-pod, tiddle ear-pod)

Zubu and Sambo got on board the overnight snake on wheels to Poneke. The long and winding train reminded them of their friend back home in Thailand. His name was Jaunty Python and he was a friendly and jolly fellow for a snake - instead of running away all the village children would run to greet him as he emerged from the jungle.

117

Jaunty would take ten or more of them at a time for a ride on his back, so big and powerful was his body. This new train-snake was jaunty too, although every now and then it let out a great roar which even Zubu and Sambo found frightening because where they came from snakes were always very quiet and moved softly so no one could hear them coming and in their two loves there is but one respect.

Still this was a new country and things were certainly different in Aotearoa. Even the reason for their haerenga was very strange and the more Zubu and Sambo thought about it the more they looked at each other in wonder and puzzlement. Why were two tigers going on a tiger hunt? And the tiger they were hunting sounded very strange indeed. It lived in the far south of Te Waipounamu and was a Scottish tiger who travelled around on wheels through the streets of Otepoti with people inside just like abus or a snaketrain or a carcat.

Something else was funny about Aotearoa. Every place seemed to have two names, one in English and one in Māori and any of these, or all, or more were the ones which Zubu and Sambo knew more of because they were the ones which Rangi and Hine had taught them in their waka under the pohutukawa trees. As the wakaneke sped through the landscape, the two tigers looked through the window skin and saw many strange things which were different to their homeland.

At one point, whilst observing the beautiful far-off mountains of the centre of the centre of Te Ika a Maui (the fact that the snake was travelling across the back of a fish was very weird to the tigers), they saw a long and winding river leading to the door of the train. Rangi had told them to beware of the taniwha which lived in every river of Aotearoa for they can suddenly swell up and kill a wakaneke just like swatting a fly. The boy told them of the taniwha of Tangiwai which did just that and which had haunted train travellers in that part of the country ever since. This reminded the tigers of the Acquatic Anaconda back home who calls on thee, let him bring forth he who causes havoc amongst the river boat travellers of Thailand.

He was a large legendary snake who rose up out of nowhere swallowing boats and barges in one gulp and disappearing back into the depths of dark waters as mysteriously as he had risen from the water. But all this thinking of their old friends made them homesick. So they summoned their waka to meet them across the road from Wellington Station as soon as they arrived, so they could fly directly to Dunedin to meet Rangi and Hine who were meeting them in their search for Roary.

Meanwhile, the two children had flown down to Christchurch to catch the ghost-train to Otepoti.

'Come on Rangi, we'll be late for the train' cried Hinengaro. The two children were on their first trip to Te Waipounamu and they were both really enjoying the new sights of the Greenstone Island. It was the first time they had been allowed to travel without adults. They were excited because they were going to see their friends, Zubu and Sambo, in Dunedin. Looking out of the window of the carriage they saw first time of the faraway beauty and grandeur of the Southern Alps.

The snowy peaks and sheer height of these mountains were unlike anything they had experienced before and they either sat quietly thinking 'O, how thy worth with manners may we sing' or went 'aeeeeeeee!!!!' when they saw something really exciting or interesting. The sound and the motion, the 'wwwooooooooooooooo' and clickety clack of the train added to the sense of adventure.

The sky was beginning to darken and the children could see rain clouds to the south as the train went clickety clack karikiti kiraki over the Rangitata river bridge and swung south-east towards the coast. The coastal cloud began to enshroud the train as it passed karikiti kiraki Orari and on down through karikiti kiraki Temuka. Rangi turned to his sister and said 'I feel like we're carrying an ancient sacred fire, e Hinengaro' and she looked at her brother and saw the serious expression on his face which sometimes got when his mind was visited by dreams and visions. She laughed and said 'You and your silly games kill me with spites; yet we must not be foes. Anyway, you know mum said to us not to play with fire!' and both of them began giggling.

Karikiti kiraki Arowhenua went whizzing by and suddenly the train was plunged into darkness as it entered a tunnel, ay me, but yet thou might'st my seat forbear, thought Hinengaro. Because there were lots of other children on the train as it was school holidays many of them were yelling out and screeming and squeeling with delight. 'Yyyiiiippppeeeeee! Wooeeaaaaaaa! EEEEEEiiiiiiiiiiiiiii!!!!'

But when the train came out of the tunnel into the light of the day Rangi and Hinengaro saw that something very strange had taken place in the darkness. The carriage had turned into a moving Marae as the train passed through the place between life and death. 'E nga mana o te rerewe, E nga reo o te tereina, E nga hau e wha o nga pahihi – Tena koutou, tena koutou, tena koutou katoa, ki kaiarahi taua he whakatupu raruraru i tënei wa' a man with a tokotoko was welcoming everybody from the many places of the world to this railway journey and urging them onwards.

The train was bolting along by the time it went through karikiti kiraki Pareora. The desolate sands and the crashing breakers heightened by the karanga which welcomed the new passengers to the train. The wero was a bit constrained because of the lack of space traditionally needed to lay the challenge in front of the manuhiri. Once the evil spirits had been sent packing by the powhiri everyone was feeling relaxed and happy on this marae o te rerewe - karikiti kiraki as the train crossed the Makikihi river bridge Rangi turned to his sister in amazement, and he thought 'but here's the joy: my friend and I are one.' Where the seats used to be now mattresses had been put on the carriage floor and the sound of the contented voices of the travellers was like an expectant murmuring of the branch of a river as everyone waited for the mihi and the whaikorero.

A waiata could be heard rising above the din of the machinery from one of the 'songbirds', the women, who was singing a lament for the once pure waters now polluted by industrial and agricultural waste. With the whole train resounding to the music of a waiata tapu Rangi and Hine were looking out the window watching a man riding a penny farthing bicycle. He dressed in a three-piece suit with a fob watch and a top hat as the train moved slowly through the town of Oamaru.

All the people of the Marae train were beginning their hariru and hongi with the people who would continue the journey further south. The whole train turned into a movement of music and magic and aroha as it suddenly went into another tunnel darkly bright, are bright in dark directed so that the waiata became the poroporoaki of the travelling Kaumatua and all the other people from the Marae train had disappeared by the time the train came out into the daylight.

Rangi and Hine looked around their carriage which had returned to its normal seating arrangements. All the carvings and mattresses had gone. The Marae atea had been replaced by the buffet section of the carriage, same as it ever was. The train was slowing down as they saw they were coming along the harbour causeway leading into Dunedin town, for nimble thought can jump both sea and land. Finally it pulled into the big, old stone station.

When they got off the train and onto the platform they both ran up to meet Zubu and Sambo, the other two, slight air and purging fire, who were waiting for them, their way lighted by a candle-aire. As they all sat inside Roary, the Tiger Tea Bus, the friends swapped stories of their collective adventures of taniwha and ghost-train marae as Roary pointed out interesting parts of Dunedin ...

Munchausen dream Number 9: 'But then begins a journey in my head, a zealous pilgrimage! Now the moon begins to shine, Goodnight, sleep tight: dream sweet dreams for you, dream sweet dreams for me.'

But Alex knew that his dreams would be anything but sweet! His night mare was beginning to ride, and she don't care.

'Right', said Fred, 'the starting-point for the investigation is provided by a fact without parallel, which defies all explanation or description – the fact of consciousness.'

Magic Alex looked at Fred and Bruno, and in an exasperated tone exclaimed, 'You two are driving me C R A Z Y.'

Fred ejaculated in a Janeayrian manner, 'Ooohhh, baaaby, you're driving me C R A Z Y, everytime I look around ...'

Bruno cast this aspersion aside and said, 'How would you like to be, under the sea i roto i te Mahinga Kai ō Te Wheke i te Maru Raiti.'

Alex said softly, 'I'd rather that you picture yourself on a train on a station, with pāua shell porters and nikau palm ties ...' and they began to see what goes on in his mind.

A spam e-mail arrived at this point (SPAM, SPAM, SPAM, wonderful SPAM ooompah, ooompah, stick it up your joompah, look at the MAPS backwards and wherever you're trying to go you get SPAM)

Good Day. I know this mail will come as suprise to you but in a brief introduction. My Name Is Miss Nidal Katmed from Sudan. I am 22 years old. It is my pleasure communicating with you for the first time and believing that it will lead to a better relationship between us. I have an inheritance that I would want to invest in your country. The amount is US$5.598.000. I want you to stand as my late father business partner in claiming the money from the security company here. I am ready to part with 15% of the total sum to you if only you assist me to claim the money and assist me also in investing the money in any lucrative business. I will give you more detail and forward all vital information as soon as I hear from you. I LOVE YOU, BUT GOD LOVE YOU MUCH. Best Regards. Miss Nidal Katmed ... **here delete, don't eat the delicious SPAM**

now here come old flat top Magic Alexis, otherwise Finnucane's fifteen, almost at hand, the cask-wine was ready to flow, the eight foot skull was ready to show: located within the particular model sat Bruno and Fred. All around the inside of the Magic's Skull, or Nothing Box, were pasted in invisible ink sentences from Magic's Munchausen memoir of his time with Apple, *Fab Four to End Yet Again.*

Only the people inside his Skull could read these illuminated manuscripts. They both wore a special pair of sunglasses to expose the magic words of wisdom: both Fred and Bruno sat in darkness between each thought, and they thought let it be. Through Magic's bi-focals the jocular profundities of the Master would gradually appear from the void, it is not dying ... it is not dying ... it is the inner light! But in the still lightless skull they both sat silently in anticipation, both intrigued and fearful at being inside the mind of their charge. Out of the darkness the first flicker of light crossed the unlevell horizon. Slowly, where landscape might have been, the first words appeared to be a dark cavern of a room with the word 'Providence' in Gothic script written on a board above a doorway, followed by the words 'let him vere to the north or other cardinal points and promptly the other by as much to the antipode.' Hoping for a little light relief after they entered what appeared to be the poorman's archway to heaven, the pineal body of Munchausen! But now the light began to in the inner sanctum of a Ha (per) bizarre where anything goes, to the tune of goth and ghoul music – any old way you choose it! As their eyes gradually became accustomed to the darkness Bruno and Fred saw that the mind they were in was decked out with many sheets of black plastic, the only lighting powered by Watt began to re-emerge. This time the thoughts were theirs as well as being Alex's and were of a landscape devoid of colour as the landscape of lessness: 'by degrees less dark till final grey or all at once as if switched on grey sand as far as eye can see beneath grey cloudless sky same grey.' Fred and Bruno stood around as though they were in some other-worldly trance. The predominant colour of attire was black, with blood-red and sometimes white silk scarves making up the affected effect. Ignoring the nobles' propaganda concerning peasants, there was a definite air of egalitarian elitism at the gathering darkness. And the Munchausen Alex in the newly returned darkness grieves for the love he has forsaken in return for what he thought would be intellectual and spiritual enlightenment. He longs for the warmth and tenderness of intimacy and the small trials and successes of ordinary human life. But the womb-like darkness disappears, and despite the overriding feeling of sombre nihilism there were touches of humour and eccentric camaraderie like any kinky Loyola citizen La La La La Lola. The gloom room reveals its past: 'said pale as dust. Ah, but dust indeed deep to engulf the haughtiest moments which too it once was here and there.' (Chicken Maaaaaan! He's everywhere! He's everywhere!) with an inscription 'Henry the Fowler II' hung around his neck, his pince-nez sitting unsteadily on his beak, somewhere between the Scylla and Charybdis of the hollowcause to which he aspired. Doc Bloch, Geli the black Jenny of schoolgirl fantasies, beautiful! My Aachen heart black stockings disappearing under the shortened school uniform of desire, now with the white ghostly visage and thick black lips of my dying bride, is it any wonder that I have faith no more in the system of existence called life! 'Bone white of the sheet seen from above and the shafts fore and aft and the dwarfs to the crowns of their massy skulls.' Small stars were shooting as Fred and Bruno, the wishful thinkers yelled, and there was an uneasy shiver of laughter inside the skull. Out of the place whence the ice emerged stepped a wizard-like figure who introduced himself to those assembled as 'The Master of the Side Real Pendulum.' The Furher's speech somehow sent the secretion of Alex's thoughts into convulsions from before backwards to the conical cone of his tip-topsy pineal popsy curvey, 'Te Ra ö Ngä Mate, nö Reira' he thought.

Again he lost his A E I O U twenty-dollar note and his thoughts became distracted and d's'm'v'll'd, albeit brfly – in shorts, he had emptied his vowels! 'Same grey all that little body from head to feet sunk ankle deep were it not for the eyes last bright of all.' Suddenly the ambiance of the Gothskullroom changed to a quieter, more subtle mood as Bruno changed the music on the CD player. The soft, seductive voice of Celine Dion permeated the air, like a religious hymn, with the song, 'D'un Chateau l'autre', from her latest album, *Voyage au bout de la nuit*. The beauty of the singer's sound somehow matched the starkness and anarchy of the lyrics, the German testicular, was seen to wipe his battle-hardened eyes. A mood of heiterkeit descended upon the previously agitated, yet novel, gothic scene where even a monk or a peacock would not seem out of place. 'Breath has not left him though soundless still and exhaling scarce ruffles the dust. The reflective reverie was broken. Marilyn Manson replaced Celine and the rhyme of reason was sent riding: 'though it knows yet another end beneath a cloudless sky same dark it earth and sky of a last end if there had to be another absolutely had to be' for they were free from interference or withered murder inside Alex's Skull, whose sentinel was Wolf. The music became loud and frenzied. Bruno and Fred downed a drink and both felt the fire-laden fumes make an incision through Alex's corpus collosum, before shooting back to the centrum ovale majus, bejasus, Henry the Fowler, RF-SS, and Wolf the Howler saw the Disco Duck of St. Helena rock, and looked around for a way out of this Satan's salon. But the Sultan's swing was still sure, although shaky enough to knock over a salt cellar which bode nought but bad luck for the assembled, which now included sapphics and alcaics. 'For to end yet again skull alone in a dark place pent bowed on a board to begin.' Alex could no longer countenance the Gothic spectacle of self-creation and destruction which this part of his brain was experiencing. The fear of fire in his pineal gland in the hand led him to seek refuge in a neutral precinct. Around his neck was a momento from the thousand seconds' riot he had just attended – a silk scarf which he felt soft and sensual yet somehow menacing against the lower regions of his anterior surface, like a large noose made from silken piano wire ... backs to the skull the motherfuckers of the literati small chat as they pigswill casks and champ at the bits of cheese and almost crackers Finnucane, nee Fred and Bruno, can no longer contain themselves, asking is the monkey who wrote Shakespeare the same one who ate cheesecake?. Në Dada 'he waved aside with a sweeping, somehow inclusive, gesture, a sombre pillar advancing bearing a tray of chocolate skulls' passing them around. Anxious, for the show must go on, Alex takes one in his hand and in a mode of benediction uplifts the host-like choc-skull, as though it is a whole being and places it into his open maw. As he bites the delicacy he feels an almost imaginable crunching sensation and hears or seems to hear a silent cry, a final breath expiring. A thin trickle of raspberry coloured liquid runs slowly down the tiny canals of his mouth towards his chin, and he thinks, and only thinks, he tastes the uncertain lick of blood. Baffled and perplexed the shadow thrown over the trio by the large skull has lifted. Turning around as one, they see nothing but empty space, skull last place of all black void within you without you till all at once or by degrees this leaden dawn at last checked no sooner dawned ... what did you kill?

(all de children sing) how does it feel to be one of the beautiful people now
Refrain: *Cuesto obrigado tanta mucho que* can eat it, *carousel*

Magic Alex sat in his lonely cell phone, a captive of his own genius. All the secrets and inventions in his 'Nothing Box'; a sealed cube with randomly-blinking lights, a skull, had now become common currency, haunting him like a perpetual nightmare. 'I'm on the train, now' said one of the millions of messages his cell-phone prison communicated. 'I'm on the train, again and again and again' ... he gave himself a wan, ironic smile as the last text message for the evenimg arrived from his girlfriends who wiggled their little titties in a goodnight in a life affirming wave as seen on his little screen to the sound and rap hip-hop vision, **'HPYROK, GDNT, LUVU, A&J,'** the world had become the 'virtual reality' he had envisioned after a long paranoid trip and every night was the same, the drug-train, the Dreamlander Express, entering the tunnel of his soul – everything ...

(all de children sing) we were the coming generation
(all de children sing) we were going to be the world's salvation
(all de children sing) now the legacy of da baby boomer
(all de children sing) is a society of conspicuous consumer
Between the the glitch and the gremlin falls the MACHINE
Between the systemic failure and you and me falls the mean
There may not be much difference between Hitler and the Pope
If we give them both a smoke of dope and a piece of rope
Hitler was a Catholic and the Pope was a Hitler Youth
And a wasteful rubbish dump of dumbed down thoughts
The opium of the people, a penny for the old guy of yer thoughts
(all de children sing) it so often ends in a cancerous tumour
(all de children sing) the second coming is a baseless rumour
(all de children sing) what's the point of a song without humour
(all de children sing) and Alex's magic turns him from man to ... birdwing (oozingooooozingwooooozing) out like the jampacked jackbooted blackhole of calculated-cutoff, sick from laughingcrying his tragic but very catholicandirishmaori deathof superstitious love now the hawkis flying madlytrying toget level withwhat heseesis nowan on comingtrain a fast traincoming, birthdaybarb (64), forhe hashada vision of himself, a burnt out hard-case from the Hippie generation, lost in the space of his own thoughts, sinking in the quicksand of his thoughts, wandering internally as Ghostly Himmler had sunk and wandered in his own ghastly dream-reality, we should have listened to John, the dream is over, all the ex-LSD Treasury boys, and the Waffen SS boys, all those who have flown so high likea hawkin the snow no nohues only black and whitein the night and himselfon the train thinking through the NICP of the NIMT, haurangi, hawkhas vision of death, not bloodymurder but bloodystupid falling from the traindrunk and the manhimself coke in hand woowoowoowoo trainlurches forwardback and the hawkis alongside as the dooropens ina flash of bird blinding light the himself hawk sees himself standing at the doorway train of thought lurches back unstable on feet too much whiskey toomuch craic dangerwas in the air as the hawk who had flowna longway the wrongway in time and distance headedfor the train the light from the vestibule shining in hiseyes and he could see the startled uncomprehending drunken gaze of himself ... and

he, Alex, was Rubezahl as he launches his nightly 'myspace' entry into cyber-space, and spoke to himself the more external communication you make the less communication there is ... his last 'Munchasen Moment' for, in the end ... the love you take is equal to the love you make ...

EPILOGUE

'Mein Name ist Rubezahl Munchausen' the dream #9 proclaims
For many centuries he lived on the outskirts
Of towns and villages near the Black Forest
And one of his names means Ghost of the Mountains

His dark hair and beard made him mysterious
And people would fear and revere his image
In 1944 he left his ancestral home
Haunted by the darkness and anarchy which reigned

Rubezahl could no longer travel as a spirit
For the world had made him worldly
By the time he left old Germany
So he escaped in a U Boat wolf-pack

Not used to temporal confinements
And restrictions of the human body
His aparition roamed restless from country to country
Afraid of nothing but his own fears

At nights whilst he wandered some foreign road
The moon and stars shining in his brain
His heart would be reminded of the pain
Caused by loneliness and separation

Rubezahl Munchausen carried the burden of guilt for his people
Though no one he met ever knew this
But there was not a woman he could kiss
And not feel that he was a deceiving Judas

At the half-century he arrived as a not-born baby
In the remote southern land
Nothing more than an embryo, a bland
Homunculus in his Earth Mother's womb

Rubezahl Munchausen arrived early and so
Was a little unsteady on his feet
His understanding of things was incomplete
And education just confused the issue

So with a child's mind he tried
To understand why he didn't belong
Why he felt unusual, why all wrong
Amongst these foreign people, his family

Once Rubezahl Munchausen was playing war with other boys
And he wore the symbol of the broken cross
The swastika, he was the Kommandant, the boss
But his Earth Father told me off, saying he could be arrested

Later Rubezahl Munchausen's Earth Parents died
Other people tried to tie him down
But he felt threatened and thought he would drown
In the sea of human obligation

He moved southward on a journey of discovery
He went to a place which was neither here nor there
It was in this strange stone city where
They told him why he didn't belong

One day Rubezahl Munchausen stood on a mountain
Snow was falling on the surrounding rocks
The cold went to his bones - a memory unlocks
In his mind, a vision of the Black Forest in winter

'Am I evil', Rubezahl Munchausen wondered, his *Schuld*
And this thought drove him on like a demon
The darkness inside him fuelled further the notion
As he moved away from the life around him

Three women teachers came to him, old and young
Dark and light, friend and lover
With each of them he would discover
Something of himself and his loneliness

One of the three tried to awaken Rubezahl Munchausen as a human
'You are just ordinary', she said
'For a while it is with you I want to be'
But he was afraid of her words and love

The next one was his blood sister
'Come on', she said, 'let's go brother
To find the ancient land of our father and mother'
He hugged her close and said goodbye

On a windswept suburban railway platform
The old woman looked at him and said
'Rubezahl, Rubezahl', like a voice from the dead
And the past before the past opened up before him

What now for this Rubezahl Munchausen and his *Schulden*?
Who took on human form so he could live
Only now it is too late to return to the spirit
Rubezahl Munchausen will die and alone and haunted

With the irony of love following him for eternity
His mind will be his Black Forest now, *Abnobae
Jugo*, he's Avienus the poet, who fears what he reveres
With the new beginning of the Eternal Recurrence

The mist closes around the Munchausen Ghost of the Mountain
The mist behind which he hid all those centuries

www.ingramcontent.com/pod-product-compliance
Lightning Source LLC
Chambersburg PA
CBHW060635130626
46555CB00002B/809